I dedicate this book to a fellow medium, who is not only exceptionally talented and gifted but works with no ego, only truth, honesty and to help heal the hearts of many. This amazing lady has faced such hardships throughout her life which most would not know, enabling her to resonate and empathise with others. She only seeks and speaks the truth which, at times, can offend those who don't like honesty. I wish there were more people like you in the world, Marina! Thank you for being part of my journey and most importantly my friend.

THE RELUCTANT MEDIUM Part 2

Jane Lee

CONTENTS

INTRODUCTION

I thought it was worth introducing myself for those who haven't read the first book, 'The Reluctant Medium.' I didn't get to choose whether I wanted to be a medium, I was born with the ability to see the spiritual world.

I was brought up in a large catholic family where literally, if you spoke of anything other than the catholic religion it was frowned upon. I had no one to help me develop or explain why I could see, sense and feel what others couldn't.

My childhood resulted in a perpetual fear of not wanting to go to sleep at night as this was when the spiritual world would become most active and wanted to desperately communicate with me. I secretly hated my catholic school.

The hatred worsened after it was confirmed during an assembly that anyone who spoke or communicated with the spirit world was evil, which I found really upsetting at the age of five. I knew I was good, kind and loving, so why had God said I was evil?

The world I found myself in was frightening, with the sensory overload of noise and heightened emotions of others. I had no problems making friends and found the other children would gravitate towards me, wanting to share their problems, worries and fears.

At such a young age I found school overwhelming. I knew I made the other kids feel happy and safe. Ironically, I didn't know how to make myself feel safe and secure. It wasn't like I could turn around to a catholic teacher and say, "Don't want to concern you, Miss but I can see dead people." No, it needed to be kept as my shameful secret!

While I was never able to successfully eliminate my gifts, I thought I had pretty good control over them. Yes, I would still see the spiritual world and know information about others, but I learnt the ability to compartmentalise my life. I joined the Royal Air Force at seventeen, which taught me extreme discipline.

The training also made it easier for me to control my mind and distract myself from the spirit world. I also knew that if my secret ever came to light in a male-dominated environment, I would literally not last five minutes.

Whilst serving in the military, I had acquired a nasty injury and had seen and tried every medical professional and procedure. I was desperate, so when I heard about a highly recommended healer I thought, "Why not? It couldn't do any harm."

Keeping the story short and sweet, the healer unbeknown to me had opened up all my gifts – the gifts I thought I had successfully locked away. It felt like I was literally in the middle of a horror movie.

Spirits were so eager to communicate with me, it was relentless. It resulted in me doing the bravest thing I could think of, and that was keeping the bedroom light on and refusing to close my eyes until I literally passed out.

Within a matter of minutes, the bedroom would be full of shadow forms of spirit presences resulting in me screaming. I'm amazed I have been married over twenty five years! Now that's a bloody miracle.

I contacted the healer for another session, panic-stricken, I told her what had happened and begged her to take it all away. She told me, "I'm sorry, there is nothing I can do. I think you are a medium. You need to find a medium to help you." I was horrified. I thought to myself, "She can't leave me like this!

What is a medium and how the hell do I find one?" This is where I met my close friend Eddie, who held my hand throughout the journey. He was a tough, no-nonsense medium who took no prisoners.

Eddie is the last person in the world you would expect to be doing spiritual mediumship. He was a man's man, cockney accent and normal! I told Eddie I really didn't want to be a medium.

He informed me, much to my horror, that the majority of mediums have a choice whether they want to develop but I had apparently agreed to work for the spirit world before I was born(Not convinced! I'll sit on the fence for that one). Therefore I had no choice. Yikes!

Throughout my journey, on several occasions, I have tested Eddie's words by doing and trying every trick in the trade to shut off and deny my true self. To my surprise, my gifts only became stronger and more heightened. A lesson for all: you can't hide or run from yourself!

The first book 'The Reluctant Medium' explains the physical, mental, emotional and spiritual challenges I have had to overcome to be more accepting of who and what I am. In my first book, I talked about some of the most gifted, non-egotistical, kind and loving mediums who I have had the honour of working and developing with.

My journey to date has not been conventional and certainly hasn't been boring. I must mention that in the first book, I also talked about my health struggles. I was eventually diagnosed by a very well respected neurologist with a condition called PPPD (Persistent, postural, perceptual dizziness.

Google it if you are interested, it's bloody awful.) In simple words, it's chronic dizziness and is described as a constant sensation of floating or rocking. Bright lights, noisy environments and surrounding movements like passing cars can make the symptoms worse.

Occasionally, the dizziness can make you feel like you

are falling, which heightens your stress and makes your symptoms worse. Let's face it, nobody wants to fall over or look drunk in public. Hence PPPD can significantly affect your quality of life as you often find the fast pace of everyday environments unenjoyable.

To be honest, it can also become too exhausting for your brain to process, so you will need more rest throughout the day. There are treatments that can help, but no guarantees. Anyway, on a positive note, as much as some like a label, I'm not completely convinced.

I have been told by my spiritual guides my ill health is simply down to my physical and spiritual bodies being realigned and worked on in the spirit world. There is nothing I can do apart from wait for the spiritual world to finish the process, as apparently it's on a timeline. Great!

So whilst waiting, I continue to help myself by remaining positive, researching and doing everything in this world to enhance my recovery. I hang onto the fact that my spiritual guides have never let me down and I'm grateful for this knowledge, for I have a deep inner knowing there is a bigger picture. There could be a first time for my spirit team to get this wrong, but I very much doubt it.

I'm also very logically-minded and again, I'll sit on the fence until my health makes a full recovery and see how the story unravels. By the way, until now I haven't shared this unconventional view and certainly not to any medical professionals as I'm sure I'd be given even more labels. Some things in life are better kept to yourself!

When I think of my journey it makes me smile, even laugh, for at times it has been frightening, spooky, humbling, healing and loving. I finished the first book hoping that was the end of revealing anymore about my very private life, but the spirit world has decided differently, which to be honest horrifies me.

The first book in comparison to this book is pretty meek and mild. Although at the time of releasing it, I felt quite vulnerable and embarrassed. Well, I needn't have worried because what I have gone on to write is . . . how do I put it? Ten times worse and basically makes me sound mentally unhinged!

My journey continues, I've made a promise with the spirit world that I will write in one hundred percent truth and honesty. At times, I really wish I hadn't as some of what you are about to read will seem a little far-fetched and that's putting it mildly (More like ridiculous!). It is up to you, the reader, to decide if any of this is true and I'm certainly not interested in trying to convince anyone.

Would I believe this book if I hadn't lived through it? The truth is, it would definitely have opened my mind. I probably wouldn't be convinced either way, but I know I would have thought, "Thank goodness, that wasn't me!"

Well, it is me. It's my journey. At times, I have laughed and thought how lucky and honoured I am to be able to work with spirit. Other times, I have cried and become tired of feeling overwhelmed by simply being me. I accept that I am a medium, but through time, I accept more that I am Jane. I no longer apologise for who and what I am, for I am me!

Being a medium or anyone who feels different can be a little bit more of a struggle, but it's our choice how hard we want to make it for ourselves. I have one more final thing to say before you read my cringe-worthy truth and that is, hand on my heart, I wouldn't change a thing. Enjoy!

YOU CAN'T FIX EVERYONE

It's the early hours of the morning, it is pitch black and I felt a presence in the bedroom. I sat bolt upright in bed and saw a small black curly dog sitting by the door panting, pink tongue hanging out and just staring at me.

I found myself staring back at this cute dog thinking, "That's very strange, I don't usually get visited by dogs." Also, I thought I should probably be freaking out. To my surprise, I found myself fixated on his brown, gentle and welcoming eyes, we just stared at each other. Within seconds after I had the opportunity to take a good look at the little fellow, he disappeared.

Wow, that vision was held longer than usual! I've started seeing the same as when I was a 5-year-old child through my eyes as well as my mind. It's very interesting, but I'm tired and really wanted some sleep.

I went back to sleep, refusing to give it any more thought as I don't want to be up all night analysing the situation. I have become quite good at compartmentalising these experiences as overthinking strange events won't help and it achieves nothing apart from lack of sleep.

So, I happily drifted back off to sleep.

I'm now on stage in front of a huge audience wearing a bikini (This is not rocket science. Obviously, this resembles feeling vulnerable and exposed to everyone). An angry man in the audience insists that I fix him. His back is misaligned and you can see his spine is severely twisted. His pelvis has tilted out of position which is causing the whole of his upper body to twist out of line. He is shouting aggressively and demanding that I help him.

I'm wearing a white coat. I'm a chiropractor and I know exactly how to help him so I start to assess his muscular skeletal body. I manipulate his spine with such precision that his spine returns to normal, but literally as soon as it's realigned, the spine becomes crooked again.

I can't work out what I have done wrong as he should be healed. He is yelling aggressively now; his face is sweaty, twisting with venom and hatred towards me. I feel panic and fear rising within my throat for I desperately want to take his pain and suffering away. I passionately want to help. I try again, again and again with exactly the same outcome.

Why won't he heal? I must be missing something. I won't give up, but I'm now feeling out of my depth. The situation is starting to feel aggressive and you can physically cut through the hatred, anger, pain, sorrow and despair of this man. His aggressive angry eyes burrow through my soul with such anger and hatred.

Suddenly, I feel a familiar presence stroll in and sweep me off my feet. I'm given a huge hug which reduces me to feeling like a protected, vulnerable but now safe child. I can see his face, smell his odour and feel his touch as I crumble in his arms.

"Alright love, step to the side, let me deal with this." said Eddie, in his deep cockney accent.

Eddie immediately fixes the man and the disruption and scene vanishes.

"Jane, you can't fix everything. It doesn't matter how hard you try, some people choose not to be fixed, whether that is due to anger, sorrow or hatred. Some people, my love, can't be fixed. This world is an illusion; our stories are created by our minds. If the mind is adapted to seeing this journey in a certain way and has no desire to change, it is ultimately the person's wish.

This will always be the case. So much unnecessary pain is caused by ourselves. I wish I had known this when I was alive, for I didn't need to suffer and have such a tough time."

Eddie sighed. "Jane, you can't fix everyone, nor should you try." Eddie disappears. I feel comforted, blessed and once again, for a precious moment in time I was safe in the arms of an angel.

I lay awake in bed, replaying the dream over and over again in my mind. I'm desperate to hold onto the sound of his voice, the familiar smell and that unforgettable warm hug. His voice was so clear and strong and there was certainly no doubt in the message I received. You can't heal everyone!

It's important to mention to you, the reader, that when I dream it is more real than this world. Some call it lucid dreaming. I call it my dreaming, my dreams are as real as being in the real moment. I see, feel, smell and touch as we all do in our everyday waking moments.

I feel sometimes it would be nice to just pass out at night, but then when you get to be in the presence of a loved one who has passed over, I wouldn't change it for the world.

The funny thing is I had started to worry I couldn't remember Eddie's face which I knew was silly but that's how I felt. Well, I needn't have worried because his voice was booming clear and his face was so comforting. The hug I received was exactly as I remembered, so powerful, strong and yet gentle. It makes you feel truly loved and special.

So what did I take from this experience? Maybe, just maybe, I am creating my physical ill health by giving it too much attention and yes, Eddie you are right, as bloody always. I can't help everyone. Also, more importantly, you can't heal until you are ready!

Once again, Eddie had come into my life, gave me the knowledge I needed and now it was time to get on with it myself. Time to eliminate this repetitive childlike fear which is embedded so deeply. I am starting to think that perhaps this is an illusion and I have a choice to change my behaviour.

I have to mention I have a constant inner turmoil of believing I can confidently carry out the future tasks I have seen in my future. I've decided I have to put those thoughts away in a box until the task is presented before me. What those tasks are , I'm afraid they are too ridiculous to share.

BEFORE I CONTINUE

I must explain that after writing the first book, 'The Reluctant Medium' I genuinely thought, "Well, I've done as I have been asked by the spirit world and would simply go back to channel writing which is a breeze compared to this. But oh no, I've obviously not convinced enough people that I am of sound mind, so I have to write about what has happened since. After a couple of weeks of releasing the last book, I felt horrified, vulnerable and to be truthful in a bit of shock.

Why would anyone admit to such strange occurrences and especially someone who is so private? The honest answer is, in the hope it will help others. If you experience strange things, well now you know you are not alone.

Actually, it is more common than you think it is, just not discussed. I'm also intrigued to see if any of my visions will come true. Anyway, after a couple of weeks away on holiday, I find myself once again having to document new experiences and ones I have purposely hidden away.

The problem is my experiences are getting more extreme, why would I be shown and allowed to witness things others don't see, sense, feel and know to be true? I ask my guides why show me if I can't scientifically prove any of this to be real as they know I like to prove things to be real. The answer is "All we want Jane, is for you to write – nothing more, nothing less.

Time is running out, you must write. It's coming straight at you, you won't see it coming but it's coming straight at you, write." Well, that's not creepy or worrying, I think. What is coming at me? One thing I have learnt is I am one hundred percent protected, always have been and always will be until I return back to my true home.

So once again, I decided I'm going to trust! I have a knowing that it's going to be interesting, exciting and bumpy but what the heck, I like a challenge.

HOME LIFE NEEDS TO CHANGE

I have this amazing man in my life who really believes in me. I genuinely can't think of anyone else in the world that would be willing to share my life and listen to all the bizarre things I talk about openly. I'm not stupid, I have the intelligence to work out what to say and what not to say in society, that was until now!

Anyway, I digress, I have been telling Tony for the past 6 months he will be changing jobs soon. It will be engineered by the spirit world and everything is going to be alright.

Eventually, we will be creating something that will help people worldwide. As I say this to him, it feels firstly, egotistical and secondly, pretty naive and stupid but it's important he knows we will be alright. "Well, that will be exciting if that happens as the continual demanding fast pace of the commercial world takes a toll on your health and let's be honest, I'm not getting any younger. We must be realistic Jane and as you know, money pays the bills," Tony replied.

The thing with my Tony is he is such a hard worker, does everything to the best of his ability and is an all or nothing kind of person. The work-life balance has become like so many others-unhealthy. Tony is working 12 hours a day and even when he has time off, you can see he is still thinking of work. The kids adore their dad, but now we are starting to keep our daily troubles away from him so as not to add any more pressure to his life.

He is quite old fashioned in the sense that he takes his responsibility as the only male in the house to protect and provide for his girls. Equality! I hear the thoughts of many, yes, I agree but at this time in our lives it works for us, we are a team but to be quite frank, I find it very attractive and refuse to apologise.

In April 2021, Tony comes home and tells me he has taken an opportunity to leave work. Well, I knew it was coming but I didn't see it arriving out of the blue and thought we would be given more notice. I admit to Tony I'm shocked but relieved as we have all been growing further apart.

I have also been keeping home difficulties and secrets away from him as we could all see the stress, pressure and strain he had been under. Tony was really upset when he realised that we had stopped talking our problems through with him for that was always our strong point as a family.

If this opportunity hadn't arrived he would have continued to run himself into the ground as he would never give up. Tony is also ex-military so unfortunately he has a military attitude to life which is, it's ok for others to show weakness but not him.

I was secretly worried about his health because he had started to age rapidly and didn't look like his usual vibrant self. He had become lured into the materialistic fast-paced world, didn't know how to say no and had become like so many others: trapped.

IT'S GOOD TO TALK

Tony and I have these amazing conversations of what positive actions we could do for the environment, animals and humans if what I have been told by the spirit world was to come true. So, I hear your thoughts, what is it that the spirit world has shown me?

Too far-fetched at this point to share but if any of it comes true, I'll let you know. We would spend hours on conversations on what we would do if we were ever in a financial position to help others. How we could put something good back into the world.

I'm starting to sweat now as Tony has really brought into the idea that this could all be a possibility. "Right Jane, I have decided for the next few months I'm going to help you promote your work and do all the research as if we are being honest, it's not really your forte – any form of technology. (How rude!) If we want an adventure, then let's throw everything into it and see if anything happens" he told me.

Bloody hell, I hope what I have been shown happens, no pressure, my husband is going to take time off work to help me follow a very unrealistic, far-fetched dream!

I'm starting to feel a bit guilty, what if I've got all of this wrong? So, I express my concerns to Tony who says, "Jane you have been born with a gift, you know what your purpose is and what it is you need to do. Don't ever look back and have regrets, not when we have an opportunity. I would rather we had a go at something exciting than carry on with this mundane life and let's face it, it would be rather funny if you were right!" Ok but it needs to happen quite quickly as far-fetched dreams don't feed and clothe the kids.

I'm now having more frequent conversations with my spiritual team asking repetitively for reassurance. The reply I get is, you have been shown the future, trust! That awful word, trust! Well, I'm committed now and the clock is ticking. I have this overwhelming sense of urgency that a window of opportunity is to appear and I need to be ready.

So, we get to work. I'm writing 'The Reluctant Medium' and Tony is basically doing all the intelligent hard work behind the scenes. I'm amused how much Tony has completely bought into the idea I'm going to be a successful writer!

He is so logical, level headed and well balanced. I have to ask him why he has bought into it for he is a normal bloke and I can't quite get my head around his level of commitment. His reply is, "Jane, you know I don't believe in all the spiritual bollocks you come out with as I can't process it for it makes no sense to me nor do I wish to, but I believe in you."

That is the nicest thing anyone has ever said to me for it came from love. Thank goodness I married this man! I won't lie, I'm feeling really emotional. So for the next few months we jointly decide we are going to be successful with our mission and there is no room for failure.

We have already decided when we succeed, we are going to live in a particular part of England where we will be surrounded by trees and nature. Also the beach will be a 30- min drive away not too far from family and loved ones. I'm happiest when I can see trees. It fills my heart with such joy, contentment and peace. I also love the thought of a slower life, hidden away and out of sight. Trees are so important in this world, they clean the air, but more importantly, have the ability to heal and quiet our often busy minds.

We are a generation who likes to talk about mental wellbeing and how we all need to reduce our stress levels. I have found the solution, STOP CUTTING DOWN THE TREES! Create more green spaces with lots of trees so everyone can enjoy nature, imagine parks that are free for all to enjoy and don't discriminate on who you are or what you own. Prevention is better than cure and in the long run would save the amazing NHS millions.

It's so obvious, humans need nature for health and clean air, not concrete cities. Don't get me started on our seas! Another hidden topic from the public, research it! Yes, it will upset you but we all need to start taking responsibility for our planet for the days of relying on our leaders to save us are truly over. (Too preachy? Sorry!)

We schedule occasional days to visit this area so we can visualise our new life and how it makes us feel. I'm going to bore you now the reader, if there is something in this life you really want, visualise it. By this I mean see it as though you already have it, you are there.

How does it make you feel? It should fill your body with tears of happiness, love and contentment. The feeling is so powerful it feels like you have already received it; the positive energy that is released into the atmosphere is more powerful than what you could imagine.

Give it a go, absolutely nothing to lose but everything to gain and it lifts the mood. Those that are committed with this exercise and don't succumb to doubt usually succeed. Once again, I didn't think Tony would even attempt to try this but fair play to him, he is giving it a go.

After a couple of weeks of visualising our new home and way of life which might I add also has a beach hut. I have always wanted a beach hut overlooking the sea, just sat there with a cup of coffee watching the world go by. I visualise the sun glistening off the sea, people paddling and laughing with joy. I can feel the breeze upon my skin, smell the sea air and feel the warmth of the sun.

My whole body fills with joy as I feel emotional with all

the gratitude, contentment, happiness and finally inner peace. When you spend time visualising what it is you want, I can't express enough, you have to literally jump into the visualisation and be physically, mentally and emotionally in the moment. It gets easier with practise and dedication.

Anyway, this is my idea of luxury and pure bliss, my beach hut, bolt hole by the beach. Not only that, but the joy it would give my parents and siblings would be so rewarding to see. When we were growing up we always had cheap caravan holidays by the seaside and I always looked at those families who had their own beach huts in awe and how lucky they were!

It probably seems a little extreme this visualisation, but once again, I have been told I need to by the spirit world. I used to question all the time, but now if it feels right, I just go with it. I'm told the process will run smoother if I can see, sense and feel my dreams. All a bit bonkers, but not doing anyone else any harm, so why not? This proves to be more challenging than I originally thought for I'm not a fan of opulence and quite happy with what I have got. I have been brought up to appreciate what you have and find extreme wealth quite vulgar.

Why do you need more and more and more if you have enough? If you can pay the bills, feed the family and have a nice holiday each year, I feel really blessed. Also, it fascinates me that some people work themselves into the ground and end up having little time to do the things they enjoy and not even noticing the kids and grandparents getting old.

We are all led to believe this is acceptable, not having the time to notice the passing of time. But more importantly, I have met so many, so-called spiritual people who in theory should have more of an understanding, behave so appallingly for material gain.

WE TAKE NOTHING WITH US WHEN WE DIE!

So why and how are we still missing the point? I just don't get it and probably never will. I thought I was doing rather well with the visualisation of a new home surrounded by trees and having a beach hut, but no, apparently this is not good enough. I was told on 6th July 2021 that I need to work harder with my visualisations and think bigger, grander, more money, riches, luxuries, not millions, but billions! "You need to think big to be able to make a difference. This actually makes me feel horrified and repulsed.

How can you feel pleasure from something that shouts at you as wrong? But then I twist it around, if it could help others then surely this would be alright? So, I have to first research what a billion looks like on paper, 9 zeros, who would have thought! I have a suspicion I have to overexaggerate the wealth to achieve what we actually need. This is getting a little bit stupid and unrealistic so I decided to keep this information to myself, so I don't end up being sectioned.

As sad as it is, I have to give up my beach hut and swap it for a beach apartment. At first I looked at fancy apartments and homes and found myself thinking that's so huge it would be a nightmare to clean and then Tony is going to ruin that garden by the time he has finished with it! Jane, oh yes, you will be able to afford a cleaner and a gardener.

This challenge from the spirit world is probably the most difficult but I have to remind myself there has to be a good reason for all of this. I'm desperately hoping maybe I will have the honour of putting something good back into this world. I don't know how yet but I have decided not to waste any more time trying to figure it out as they will have already engineered it and I will be shown when the time is right.

So for a period of time, I visualise most days, I have found a method to include my loved ones so I can feel the love, pleasure and excitement of watching and sharing this new wealth. The enjoyment of being able to share, especially with parents that have struggled financially throughout my childhood fills me with pride and satisfaction.

I'll share my happiest visualisation with you, it's simple: I have the freedom and the time to take my mum for a dip in the sea, we can't go too far as she can't swim but the laughter and happiness, we share fills me with such emotional bliss, my whole body feels full of love. We then sipped coffee, wrapped up warmly in posh white dressing gowns, whilst sitting on the veranda of our apartment overlooking the sea.

My dad is drinking a glass of wine, giggling to himself at the realisation of being surrounded by such luxury and opulence as he was brought up in a small council flat in Penge, London. The pleasure of being able to give opportunities to normal folks fills me with pride. These feelings of love, happiness and positivity without realising it have already been sent out into the vibrational frequency or atmosphere, basically the world. The belief is so strong, it has already happened!

Thoughts are so powerful and yet we underestimate how vital they are. We have all met uplifting people who seem to have everything positive around them. Maybe they are drawing it towards them? We have all met people who are half empty and have the weight of the world on their shoulders. Unfortunately, whether you choose to believe or not, the Law of Attraction is very real.

We all have a choice, succumb to negativity or pick yourself up and work each day at seeing the positive in every situation. Only those who fight on can heal and trust me the journey is so much more enjoyable. Plus, you attract more like-minded and kind people around you. Another important tip when you visualise what you want, the more you can feel the sensation and it becomes like you are completely living it, the quicker and stronger it will become. (Crazy women? Perhaps, but worth a try!)

Towards the end of writing this book I reread this chapter and felt uneasy and frankly silly writing this manifestation chapter as I have no proof. I was considering taking it out, but I was told to leave it in. Why, what was the real reason behind it?

The words I received from spirit are below:

Jane, you have to explain

Explain to those

Who are deeply aware

There is more to this life to share

Share you must

An opinion and a view

For those who are ready to learn too

This world is an illusion

One created by the mind

The heartache and despair can in time

Be eradicated

By simply

A change of the mind.

This world is full of beauty

Happiness, love this is true

But only those who are awake

Get to truly feel, sense and see too.

All must be aware with practise each day

Phenomenal occurrences are upon us

Each day

Spiritual growth, lessons too

That will make your journey one of truth

What is the reason for time on earth?

To awaken the soul

Stop, listen and stare

For those who rush, learn very little in this life

Just a time of worry

Often heartache and despair.

We can't express enough

This journey is supposed to be full of love, kindness and care

But yet too many of you folk

Refuse to learn the lessons that are in front of you

Literally in the vibrational atmosphere

Surrounding you

In the air.

So perhaps give it a go

That's all we ask

Manifestation for everyone

The whole world

To share.

Great, now I feel even more idiotic. I wish I hadn't listened and just taken it out but I've learnt this is how it goes! Thought-provoking to those who have a deeper inner knowing there is more to this life than what we are led to believe.

The point of being here is not to chase material opulence that we can't take with us. I suspect it is to take in every experience that we feel, sense, hear and know to be of importance. Important to go back to basics and listen to our instincts.

If we all did this, we would spend more time caring for one another which would stop fueling the mental disease in the world. We would also learn to appreciate our time and to become more aware to spend it wisely with those we love and those who need our time. To be brave and create our inner wishes of perhaps creative desires. This is all starting to sound a little hippiefied, but the alternative is to continue for some, in unfulfilled situations.

I hear the thoughts of many, we all still have to pay bills. Yes, we do!

So whilst continuing in our daily lives, perhaps manifest what you want. The other question I asked spirit was why I needed to manifest such opulence. The answer was for me to learn it was okay to receive.

So many people, especially in caring positions give away too much of their energy without any thought of how this will impact on their energy. If a person feels uncomfortable to receive, I mean an exchange of material gain or time, they will become physically, mentally, emotionally or spiritually fatigued making them poorly.

I have an unhealthy relationship with receiving whether that is kind words, a gesture or even receiving a bunch of flowers.

I know this is unhealthy for I feel much happier giving my time and energy to others. I have recently with maturity started to stand back and observe.

The observation is, the more you give, the more is taken which once again depletes you. I am working on this and going forward in the future, I am fully aware this must change.

A DATE I WILL NEVER FORGET

If you are reading this book, then my first book at the very least has helped a few people. I promised myself under no circumstances would I release this book unless there was a reason to and it would help others as I have no desire to make myself sound any more of a fruitloop than needed. What I am about to reveal is ridiculous beyond belief, but it is one hundred percent true. It is up to you the reader to make your own mind up. Here goes!

The vibrational frequency, atmosphere, basically energy has been feeling denser, like wading through treacle. It just doesn't feel right to me what is going on in the world generally.

I've felt there is change coming but I'm not about to get dragged into what others are preaching for I need to make my own mind up and witness things for myself.

Apparently, there was supposed to be a spectacular event and energetic change on the 22nd June 2021 where we were all supposed to be going into a different dimensional energy.

On 19th June 2021, it was pitch black. I don't know what time it was, but I found myself sitting bolt upright in bed looking around the room. The whole room is full of data, numbers and letters that I don't recognise. When I say the whole room is full of data, I mean every ounce of air surrounding me. Billions of data, filling every ounce of the air, just floating, in the air.

I'm sat up fully awake just staring at it completely mesmerised as I have never seen anything like this before. The energy in the room feels strangely different, not spectacularly different but it has changed.

It's times like this when I wish I was a talented writer as I'm not doing the experience justice.

Lottie, my dog, is running around the house going mad scratching on my daughter's door, freaking out. Tony wakes up; I'm still fixating on this floating data which I would have expected to vanish as there is so much commotion going on.

It disappears, I'm in disbelief to what I have just witnessed but more intrigued how I was able to hold the energy so long to be able to see the atmospheric vibrations.

I don't even know whether the words I am using to explain the experience are correct. "What the hell is going on and what is wrong with Lottie?" Tony asked. "I'll explain in the morning, but one thing is for sure Lottie will not be settling tonight, so we will have to put her on the bed with us," I replied.

So, I picked Lottie up onto the bed which would usually result in her feeling safe and falling straight to sleep, but the poor thing sat up bolt right, shaking and staring around the room looking at what I presume was the floating data, that I could no longer see. "This isn't like Lottie; she is shaking.

What's going on, Jane?" Tony asked again. "You really don't want to know. I'm tired, I'll explain in the morning, but all I'll mention is Lottie is picking up everything I am seeing," I replied. Lottie sat up bolt right (Poor mite!) for at least another hour before she eventually passed out with tiredness.

Just a thought, I wonder what all the pets out there are truly experiencing when they behave out of character at night and there is no explanation for it? Makes you wonder as they can't just tell us. Animals, like some young children, are so aware of the otherworldly dimension or spiritual matters, but are usually too young to articulate or haven't got the means to express themselves.

If a child or pet is unsettled and frightened at night, always be loving, calm and patient for it can be frightening especially for those so young. One thing I will always be grateful for is when I was a young child, I would often wake up the house screaming or at times even sleepwalking and my dad would always get up out of bed and gently reassure me as he put me back to bed.

I would feel mortified and embarrassed especially if I had been wandering around the house or shouting out and then woken up and realised how I had been behaving. I would make up an excuse for my behaviour to try and reassure myself I knew what I was doing. My dad would sigh, never say a word and would just simply reassure me. My dad was a strict father, but never raised his voice once to me, whilst I struggled with my night time visitors and adventures. Thanks Dad, from the bottom of my heart.

The following day, I explained to Tony what had occurred. It's funny because as I'm telling him I wonder how many other people would be so honest and open to their partners. He says in his logical and engineering approach, "Well, Jane, that is fascinating. Obviously, I don't know what to make of what you have just told me.

But one thing is for sure and that is, I have never seen Lottie so frightened and looking around the room at something that to her was very real." I have to admit I'm so pleased Lottie backs up my crazy occurrences at night for it gives me a little more validation, if only to my husband.

Well, I know what I witnessed and that was an energetic frequency, possibly some sort of dimensional change in the world. What does this mean? The truth is I don't know, but I have been told by my spirit guides we have moved into a different dimension and we can't go back.

There has been a planetary change. What does it mean?

Some people, especially those who are more sensitive will feel out of sorts, perhaps struggle with why they are here and what their purpose is. Unfortunately, as a result they become a little more unsettled emotionally and perhaps mentally.

I can assure you this will become easier with time, but you just need to realise yourself you are actually okay. It just feels like an uncertain time on the planet at the moment due to the change. Be kind to yourself and know these feelings of perhaps insecurity and vulnerability will pass and you are not alone.

I have also been told for the next few years the world and events that will occur will feel unsettling and worrying. Not all you are fed through the media will be true. Unfortunately, a lot of what we are told is to distract us from what is often really going on. Again, a lot of this is conjured up to feed man's greed. I am told the truth will be revealed, but unfortunately this will create more unease and disruption.

So you must dig deep to see and believe there is a bigger, more positive picture. Under no circumstances are you to become fearful for this feeds a dark energy and we don't need any more of that in this beautiful world.

The bigger picture will be one of truth, maybe hard for the majority to digest, but surely truth is more important than lies. The world will settle in time and it's so important to have the individual ability to think for yourself. If you start to question, you will already see so many flaws in what we are fed.

I have been told the future is bright, it will be a bumpy ride and for some of you, you would never have believed you could have witnessed future events that you will see. But just ask yourself, "Could there be an agenda?" Trust in your instincts and know in your hearts the future is bright!

I ASKED A QUESTION

What would you think and how would you react if in the future you saw, as with many others, an unusual sighting? Imagine seeing a strange blue swirling substance moving in the sky and around the blue swirling presence are strange flying objects of lights flying by.

There are unusual spaceships that have never been witnessed by man. We are led to believe through the media that sightings are threatening and dangerous, we need to rush quickly indoors, all windows curtains and blinds must be drawn. At no cost must you look out of the window as this could result in potential blindness or even death.

The secret service and military are called in with the latest aircraft, apparently designed ages ago prepared for an event like this. Will our governments and world leaders save the day? Panic has risen, people are screaming and rushing to get home, cars are abandoned as the volume of traffic has grinded to a halt.

People are knocking one another out of the way to survive and take shelter. The weak are left on the streets to fend for themselves as even the public services are frozen in disbelief. The world is to be taken over by alien life!

Thank goodness we have advanced airship technology

that can fight back and protect mankind from these strange sightings. All news is reported only via the TV and radio for all to witness the terrible, life-threatening invasion of an alien species. All forms of other social media and devices for us to interact are brought down temporarily for our protection until further notice.

We are witnessing space like warfare fighting on our screen. We are all sitting in silence as we can't process what we are being shown through our TV screens. It's literally like a movie and incomprehensible. Before our eyes, we see beams of light fired from our military spaceships blowing up and destroying the threatening and aggressive alien invasion.

Eventually, after several huge explosions that light up the skies, we unfortunately see some of our own military warships being blown to smithereens. Finally, the fight has been won by us. The government leaders with our secret military service have saved the lives of us all from the threat of alien dimensional beings and saved the planet!

Everyone is to remain indoors until the world leaders can assure us we are all safe. Protocols and procedures will be put in place and allocated hours throughout the day where we are allowed out to work, socialise and children will be able to return to school once a date has been decided.

Due to future potential threats to earth, there will now

be a curfew until further notice. All people must remain indoors, with lights out from 9pm to 7am due to potential foreseeable dangers posed towards mankind. No need to panic as food will be rationed equally! The world leaders have saved the day and if we abide by the rules, we will all be kept safe.

Is this farfetched? Maybe!

How would you react in this situation?

Do you really believe an alien invasion with a higher intelligence superior to man and technology that we can't even comprehend would attack the planet?

If you do believe, then why has this not happened already?

Why have we not been told about extra dimensional alien life?

How come all of this was kept secret from the public?

Is it because we are not mature enough to make our minds up or could it have such consequences to financial organisations?

Are we being led to believe what we are fed day in and day out to be true?

Should we start to think outside the box and perhaps think for ourselves?

Every time you read or hear something fed by mainstream media, read it properly as so many of us just read the title.

What does the title usually create?

Fear, depression, anxiety and often despair.

I challenge you all to be a little more open-minded with what feels right to you.

What is your opinion?

Maybe research for yourself, the truth is fascinating!. Yes, at times a bit upsetting, but I personally prefer the truth to lies, as lies can unfortunately control how we think and behave. Fear is a dark energy this world needs uplifting and light, so dig deep and see the positive in every situation however hard it might appear. Energy and vibrations are very real, so the more positive thoughts we can send into the world the better for everyone.

So is the above example really that far-fetched, only time will tell. We would never have believed a virus would cause lockdowns and that in some countries it would be mandatory to be vaccinated. This all sounds, I'm sad to say, familiar to past historic dictatorships. What leader can you remember that removed choice from humans?

The point of this is? We all need to start thinking for

ourselves, make our own educated decisions, otherwise it really is quite a concern for the future. As I have already said, the next few years will be bumpy and at times create unnecessary fear but it's up to us to believe, feel and sense a positive outcome.

Stay true to your values of kindness, sharing, gratitude and love. The world will become a more honest, open page and more importantly, more truthful place for all to see..

AN UNSETTLING OCCURRENCE I STILL STRUGGLE TO PROCESS

I'm used to strange occurrences at night and often become a bit disappointed and bored if I haven't witnessed something unusual for long periods of time. I have a thirst to understand these events and have them explained to me so I can learn and develop my understanding of what shall we call it? Otherworldly dimensions!

I'm okay with seeing as this is my main strength, not so keen on hearing, but tolerate it and I must admit, I'm scared shitless when things become physical. I've mentioned before they can keep that paranormal creepy stuff away from me!

Unfortunately, for some reason there seems to be a pattern throughout my life as soon as I've got my head around one discipline, another closely follows to push my development. I can't and never will understand why some mediums choose to search for paranormal activity.

I get it, if you want to help a trapped soul or put something positive into the world or release something from this world for the greater good, but not just for thrill seeking adventure.

This is especially true if your intention is not honourable. I can assure you, you are not fully protected as much as you kid yourself. Dabbling with energy for self-gain and not to benefit anyone other than the thrill of your adrenaline levels is how do I put this politely, oh yes, really selfish and stupid. There are and always will be people who sneak into known haunted, historic buildings to experience paranormal activities.

The sad thing is some of these people know how the spiritual world works, even work helping heal the hearts of those who are desperate to know their loved ones are safe in spirit. Unfortunately, for some reason, others just can't resist the thrill of messing with certain energies. I suppose it's not for anyone to judge, but I'm ashamed to say I do.

If you are born and chosen to work with spirit, it is an honour although it doesn't always feel like it. So for goodness sake, stop messing around playing silly buggers and do something good with it!

Every experience I am given is sent to me because I like to think for a bigger reason which is yet to be discovered. Under no circumstances will I EVER choose to play with dark energy and certainly not for entertainment and the adrenaline rush. I don't know what events I will be asked to do in the future, but I know my team well enough to know it will benefit others.

I digress so what is it I'm putting off telling you? Here

goes, 20th July 2021, I am woken up in the early hours by a sharp pain under my tongue. I think nothing of it and fall back into a light sleep. I'm woken again, but this time lying on my back with my mouth wedged open and I can't close my mouth. It's as though my jaw has locked.

The strangest thing is I don't feel panic stricken and seem to be compliant. A metal probe is then inserted into my mouth which I can physically feel. The best description of how this felt is when the dentist places an X-ray plate into your mouth under your tongue and it pinches the piece of skin under your tongue. The probe felt too big and kept pinching the flap of skin under the tongue as if physically pinching me.

The device was finally inserted and then I felt something slither under my tongue and disappear into my body. At the same time, I felt a sharp stabbing pain in my fourth right toe. Then everything returned to normal. Yes, I've just admitted to that! I'm lying in bed fully awake thinking, "Did you really have to show me that and why as no one would believe me." I have so many questions and I know I will have to ask the following day.

So, the following day I'm eager to understand what the hell is going on and need to make some sort of rationalised conclusion.

I'm not a person who just accepts spiritual paranormal activity without an explanation. I need and want to understand. I feel more content and generally happier if I have an explanation. Once I have a logical explanation, I can process it, even if I'm not overly excited by the event, but at least I can move on. I need to understand, that's why I still miss Eddie terribly.

I would first ask my spiritual guides for explanations, then to confirm what I had been told, I would turn to my trustworthy and very honest, at times too honest friend, Eddie.

Their explanations always matched but it was comforting to be reassured in the physical world. Just being able to share my often crazy world with a very gifted medium who under no circumstances would appease me, brought me huge comfort.

I have never met anyone who can answer my questions with such knowledge and truth. I have good friends who listen, but no one can answer my often extreme and bizarre questions for they haven't had the same experiences or gained the knowledge by witnessing things for themselves.

Eddie, if he didn't know, wouldn't just answer with maybe solutions or make something fit symbolically. He would go off and ask his spiritual team and always come back with the right explanation. How do I know he was always right? Because when I'm given truth and honesty, I have a strange sensation that runs down my body–from the top of my head to my toes.

To me, this confirms that however ridiculous the answer is, it's true. Basically, I'm pretty good at knowing if someone is bull shitting! How lucky was I to have such a selfless teacher. As with all things in life, we never fully appreciate what we have until we lose it. I often send thoughts to Eddie asking him to hurry things on as I know he will be busy working with many others on the other side.

His skills will not be wasted for he always helped mediums whilst he was alive. I have no doubt he will be continuing his work finely perfecting the connection between the two worlds.

Now with no Eddie to ring, I have to trust solely on my spiritual guides for all the answers. I trust my team one hundred percent for they have never and will never let me down. The problem is I don't always believe a hundred percent in myself due to like so many others a lack of self-confidence. But it's time to push the boundaries and move forward.

I don't think I'll ever be an overly confident person. However, I refuse to let it hold me back. I, like many others, suffer with my hidden inner turmoil and anxieties, especially talking openly about my hidden spiritual gifts. However I'm determined to see where this story ends. More importantly, I want to know why, how and when good will come from all of this.

I can't believe I've been given all this shit if it wasn't for a much bigger and positive picture. Plus, my team has shown me the outcome so I want to prove to myself, all of this is not mumbo jumbo!

Another thing I forgot to mention, well, actually I didn't want to discuss, was I woke up the following morning with four small, roughly one centimetre in size circular bruises on the inner side of my upper arm close to my armpit. The bruises looked like they had been physically placed with precision. I have no recognition or explanation or felt any pain when it occurred.

I even found myself showing family members who were really shocked and asked how I hurt myself. I would reply that I honestly didn't know. They would look amused as to question why there was no way I couldn't have known? I wanted to show people almost to prove without saying anything that something strange was going on and needed to see their reaction to confirm this was a little bit outside of normality also for perhaps confirmation at a later date.

I asked the spirit world for an explanation and was shown in my mind's eye a metal looking device with a circular head like the top of a shower head. On the end of this device that looked like some sort of probe was a further four fast spinning small circles.

The device was placed into my arm and needles released in a fast-vibrating circular punching movement. Not best pleased with this explanation as it's all getting a little bit like something out of a far-fetched artificial intelligent creepy movie!

So, I finally sit down and write and I'm told I'm correct but not to over analyse and just accept the process. As for the thing placed under my tongue this has been inserted for, their words, 'words of wisdom and to relay with calmness and control.' Well, I think to myself that would be useful for I do get overanxious and speak fast when under pressure. Anything to reduce stress I suppose.

I always look for the positive in every situation for what would be the alternative, especially in my life. I'm so bored with feeling ill and physically off balance that I'm past caring and amusingly not bothered anymore. Bloody hell, it really makes me laugh how far I have come!

I genuinely don't care as long as it's explained and they get me better so I can enjoy the journey, WHATEVER! So, I'm feeling optimistic because surely things are going to improve.

After that strange event, my sensitivity to sound and noise becomes almost unbearable. My head feels like it is expanding larger than the dark room I am seeking solitude in. The pressure is unbearable and literally feels like my brain is going to shatter into a million pieces. I feel genuinely scared for my life. Why is this happening?

It's cruel! I've done everything to help myself improve. I've even become a vegan! I'm sad because I can feel myself going backwards which is heartbreaking for I've been improving. I speak to my guides who reassure me it's all part of the process and all of this is on a timeline.

I will get better and I must trust. I tell them I don't want to do this anymore, I'm tired. I even resort to telling them they can all f... off and I'm turning my back on them. They know as well as I know, I can't run away because I've tried before and it only comes back and usually stronger. A valuable lesson I must share is, you can't run away and hide who you really are for the truth always eventually surfaces to the top.

Trust me, it's easier to take baby steps forward and go with your truth, however uncomfortable and cringe-worthy it might feel.

I find myself having to spend longer times lying in bed which really upsets me, accepting I need to succumb to the process. I receive healing energy which consists of fluid being released from inside my head and comforting warmth around my lower back. I can feel the fibres within certain muscles in my body being manipulated and the jaw and neck being worked on.

I plead for them to send someone, something down to finish off the process for I know they can finish off this process quickly if they choose. From all the healing I have received and witnessing the process, it would be dangerous to rush, but why so long? Maybe so I could have a hilarious fun time writing about it so to share with others. That's lovely, but enough is enough! It really doesn't matter how much I choose to moan or plead.

I also know this process has been engineered to perfection and is on a timeline. I will not be fully recovered until the time is right. I console myself by reassuring myself how lucky I am to know I will get better and to stop moaning for there are millions of others suffering a lot worse and to man up!

So, it's back to my disciplined mind set off telling myself once again it will get better tomorrow and reminding myself of all the wonderful things I can do, how far I have come and how strong I am. The thing is I know I sound deluded, yet I also have such a strong knowing all of this will pass. I'm hanging on to this feeling for dear life and not going anywhere near the alternative.

The alternative is to go to the depths of despair and darkness which achieves nothing, only self-loathing and misery. I refuse to visit the darkness of desperation, pain, distress and hopelessness. I've already visited this world and it's stifling, like swimming through treacle struggling for breath, running out of energy, panicking and searching for a way back to the surface to finely take a large breath of air. No! No! No! I'm hanging onto trust and hope, I've learnt it is only me that can take away hope and that is not an option.

A PLEASANT HEALING

I won't lie, I'm not allowing myself to succumb to feeling out of control with the depths of despair, but I'm struggling. I went to the chiropractor, reiterated that the pain is coming from my left shoulder girdle, rib which if corrected will release the jaw, neck and left side of the body. The chiropractor who is a strong character listens, but now I need her to hear.

She really is a fantastic chiropractor and if I didn't believe she could help, I wouldn't waste my time. I send up a thought asking my guides if they can work through her or at least steer her to aid my process. I'm not sure I'm allowed to ask this or whether it is possible, but I'm tired and decided 'what the heck.' After the usual treatment of several cracks and manipulations, I decided to plead with my team.

Well, that didn't work! I thought I was being cheated out of an opportunity to move forward. Just as I get up the chiropractor says, "Jane, can you lie down again? I want to try a different approach on you." She sticks her fingers into my left armpit and moves her fingers with such precision, I literally feel shooting pain. I can't decide whether to scream or pass out. As she moves her fingers, I can feel something subtly being released. It's not spectacular, but it gives me hope.

The next day, I woke up pissed off because I've now got

a severe headache, left shoulder pain, and my armpit is throbbing. For goodness sake, make this end, I've had enough! I know I am going to get better so why all this suffering and misery? It's not like I have a desire for self-sacrifice to save the bloody world! I'm now fighting with myself to remain positive and remind myself how lucky I was before I had my armpit played with.

The throbbing is relentless, the headache unbearable and I really don't know what to do with myself. I decided to lie down. I go into a meditative state allowing my breathing to soothe the tension in my body. Within a few minutes, I feel a beautiful warmth touch my chest and heart area. A heat so gentle, yet so strong that radiates down to my lower abdomen.

I'm thinking I really should take the dog out before the kids get home but the warmth is so comforting I don't want to move. Then I feel a stronger heat within my chest that feels like an internal flame heating me from the inside out. It is the most comforting, soothing, beautiful, loving experience to date I have ever had the pleasure of feeling.

I feel so overwhelmed not just by the physical touch but the strong sensation of love. This is a time I really wish I had the ability to articulate with words how honoured, blessed and privileged I am. Tears are streaming down my face for I feel so loved, nurtured and accepted. I thank whatever it is that has shown me such kindness and healing for I am left speechless by the desire on the other side to ensure I fulfil my chosen path.

There is no doubt in my mind I will complete whatever it is I have to do, for why else would so much time, effort and love be invested in me? Lightbulb moment, I also identify that no amount of chiropractic treatments are going to sort my health out, perhaps keep me functioning and psychologically make me feel I am doing something to aid the recovery.

I suppose this gives me a sense of some sort of control and enables me to believe I am contributing to my destiny. The reality is I won't fully recover until the time is as I have been told exactly right and I also know and have always really known it will be the above that fixes me. The healing capabilities from this higher loving intelligent force are so superior to the limited knowledge of man.

We really are quite insignificant in the big scheme of things and yet so arrogant and disruptive to the world and each other with what little knowledge we are taught to believe is correct. I have hope in mankind for as I have already admitted previously the times are changing.

People are waking up, seeing the reality and the truth, finally thinking and seeing for themselves. Exciting times! Yes, the world will become a little crazy, but love and light will prevail!

Now I can hear some of you thinking, stupid woman she

is just having a hot flush and thinks it's a divine energy, bless her! Trust me without going into too much personal detail, I know what a hot flush is!

Anyway, after this event, my symptoms calmed back to their original state and I'm feeling optimistic and decided I want to see where this journey leads me and I have to learn to trust!

THE FIRST RELUCTANT MEDIUM
BOOK IS RELEASED

There is no turning back now, on the 5th of Aug 2021, 'The Reluctant Medium' book is released into the world. I have found the whole experience of writing it, exhausting yet strangely enjoyable and therapeutic. I'm feeling incredibly vulnerable for what I have written is so personal, truthful and if we are being honest, easy prey for ridicule.

I decided to comfort myself with the knowledge that unless it is successful, nobody will know it is me for, I have hidden my identity. You'll find no pictures of me on social media, for I have no desire to share my private life with others and it amuses me why others feel so strongly to share their lives with often strangers for weren't we all taught not to talk or be over familiar with those we don't know?

I'm going on holiday soon and have an overwhelming desire to hide myself away. It has taken a lot of courage to release the first book, 'The Reluctant Medium,' for it's my truth. I keep fluctuating between relief that it has finally been finished and gone out to I want to hide away and overwhelmed with feelings of complete horror.

It amuses me how extreme my desire not to draw attention to my true self still has such a strong hold over me. I admire those people who have learnt not to care what others think.

I desperately want not to care, as I know good and kind people don't judge. A few bad apples create fear of ridicule and let's be perfectly honest, nobody wants to be associated with a rotten apple.

I've already been sending out weekly channelled writings from my two previous books on social media, 'Mystic Moments in Love and Light' Vol 1 and Vol 2 which have been received with positivity and kindness. I originally declared the writings have been channelled from spirit, but haven't overly promoted this point.

I think generally people cope better when they think they are reading a thought provoking and uplifting writing from a normal writer. Tony has pointed out the inevitable 'The Reluctant Medium' needs to be promoted on social media. I'm not keen, but also know there is no point writing a book if you aren't going to share it.

So, we pay for an advertisement to promote the book. I have absolutely no idea what to expect and decided to release it just before we go on holiday.

We fly away to Cyprus which feels wonderful for I have this constant nagging and anxious feeling within that I desperately need to escape. I noticed my behaviour and realised I'm trying to run away from what I have just released into the world, my truth! "Too late now, Jane, you are committed, what have I done?"

The apartment and facilities are perfect, out of sight, private, quiet and finally I start to feel safe and breathe. This holiday couldn't have come at a better time and the simplicity of the sea air and time with the family is my heaven. I feel alive, happy, calm, so thankful and loving life.

After a couple of days, we decided to check if there are any responses to the advert we have sent out. Gosh, there are loads! I didn't realise anyone would be interested. The majority of written comments are positive and the penny starts to drop about how time-consuming social media can be and that it's not really for me.

We left it for a couple of days. Now I find myself wanting to check social media for it has a strange way of drawing you in and making you want to hear strangers' views. Why would anyone care what someone who doesn't know you, thinks about your work?

The answer is, I don't know, for I normally couldn't give a damn, but now because it is in black and white, I'm starting to care.

Here we go, the nasty comments start to come in from strangers on social media. How evil I am for there is only one book of truth, the Bible! "Nice, I bet your parents are really pleased with how well you have turned out, NOT!" Another pleasant joke about how you should punch the medium in the face, all quite charming.

I then noticed it was predominantly men passing aggressive, nasty and rude comments. I was expecting some negative comments, but was shocked, saddened and made to feel like a bad person. I was more amused by how I had let some weak, damaged, insignificant arseholes hiding behind a keyboard with obviously too much time on their hands bring me down. I was honest with Tony and expressed my feelings.

We laughed, joked and made light of the situation. Then Tony said, "Jane, you were in the military for fourteen years. You have met such a variety of characters and the so-called banter you have experienced will put you in good stead. Don't let a weak character put you off your dream." Gosh, I love this man! He always knows exactly the right thing to say when I'm having feelings of self-doubt.

I have worked with intelligent, and respected men/women in my previous career and let me mention they who are strong, don't hide behind a keyboard throwing childish and venomous comments. I have spent years in often hostile situations with some of the most interesting, diverse and brutally honest strong characters who if they had a problem with you would mention it to your face and not behind your back or on a keyboard.

If anyone behaved so cowardly or weakly, they would be utterly ridiculed and ostracised. I forgot to mention I have also been throughout my life bullied by some of the best and survived. The interesting thing I have learnt on my journey is, everyone has a choice. I have seen those who have been bullied go on to behave in the same manner and others that have broken the cycle.

I imagine lots of trolls have been bullied. I am sorry for your inner turmoil but nobody, I repeat nobody, has the right to inflict misery on others. BREAK THE CHAIN!

So, I'm not even going to entertain a person hidden behind a keyboard who is probably sitting in a little room by themselves. The image I have in my head of these sad, unkind people who are trying to bring misery to others suddenly reduced me to a smile for I can't imagine they will be of any substance.

The average person can't be bothered and hasn't the time or the inclination to behave horribly. I decided I shall send positive thoughts and healing energy in the hope it will eventually burst their bubble of self-loath and finally they will be able to add something positive to this world.

I can honestly say I had never given any thought to bullying on social media. Yes, I had heard about it because it is talked about enough on the TV, but I had never taken it seriously.

I also worry for those who have been subjected to harsh, vile and unkind words on social media. I like to think of myself as quite a strong person, but even I felt hurt, scared and sad at some of the comments. So to all those sensitive, kind and loving souls, just remember you are putting so much goodness back into the world and more important what we all need the most, kindness.

Do not succumb to self-doubt and fear for this will hinder not only yourself but others for we are all interlinked.

The year 2021 can appear a strange time in life. The world seems to be becoming a little erratic, but only if we fuel the fire with fear and darkness. We all have to lift our positive vibrations higher to ensure the future continues to shine bright. One more thing, the future is bright, but just needs a little help on the way.

THE PASSING OF TIME

Whilst we were on holiday, we had some sad news that my brother's dog had died. Bella, the boxer, had a wonderful life, but towards the end you could see she had become frail, old and tired. Whilst my brother was on holiday with his family, Bella became sick. She was taken to the vet who confirmed she wasn't going to last much longer and was given some medication to keep her comfortable until they could travel home.

Shortly before they were to return home, Bella became worse so once again, they took her back to the vet. The vet told them it was the right and kind thing to do and let her go. Bella was carried outside beneath a beautiful blossom tree and laid upon the grass, surrounded by her family. It was a gorgeous sunny day, the skies were clear blue.

Bella was always at her happiest in nature. As Bella looked up into the sky, the family each in turn, whilst stroking her soft fur and holding her paws, said their goodbyes. Bella was calm, happy and held by the people who had nurtured and loved her since birth. She fell asleep in their arms and passed simply onto another world.

I felt so sad for the loss and heartache my brother's family experienced. Those who have owned dogs will know it isn't just an animal, it is a member of your family, like another child of your pack. Bella had received so much love whilst she was here and I have no doubt is very happy where she is now.

The point of this story is sometimes it takes the passing of a loved one to make you realise the passing of time. A time to reflect on how precious our lives are. It's time for us all to stop and notice the children growing up so quickly before our very eyes and the ageing grandparents.

Time stands still for no one. Love every minute of every hour of every day. The wise notice the changing of the seasons, people and the surroundings. So many of us rush through this world jumping from one situation to another, forgetting the most important lesson, which is to stop and stare.

We live in a beautiful world with a variety of amazing people and yet so many of us become consumed by unfortunately what we are led to believe will fulfil us—success, money and more materialism. It always amuses me how as a species we often get this wrong.

Yes, we all need money to provide for ourselves, but surely not at the expense of wasting a life in search of more than we need. When we die, I like to say, pass over, we take nothing with us. Nothing! Was a life spent chasing opulence worth it?

Time is so precious, yes, it's about feeling fulfilled but also about having the time to acknowledge the changes especially if you are fortunate enough to have children. I know of so many children who have everything financially and materialistically, but are craving time and love. We have allowed society to dictate what we think is right and what is best for our children.

What do you think? Another controversial question I'm going to throw into the mix. Can we really have it all, fantastic careers, amazing home lives and content happy children? Some people don't have a choice as we have to pay bills and put food on the table.

This question is to those who have the financial ability to choose. What is more important: success, power, status or a well balanced and loved young person? I can hear and feel uproar! Good, then it has made us all think. Nobody gets everything right, yet I feel we as a species are not always even trying to get it right. Think for yourself, but don't kid yourself we can have it all. We can have it all, but at whose expense?

There will always be someone who has to make a sacrifice. Just an opinion, makes you think though, we all need to start maybe not conforming and deciding what is best for everyone. I have to clarify, yes, I am writing this book, but I am also strongly led to what I will write about and I will often receive some strong teachings from the spirit world.

This is not an excuse for what I have written and I'm certainly not backtracking for I actually agree. This sad news of the passing of Bella has taught me not only to appreciate the passing of time but to embrace my future. Face all my fears, own my challenges and grow from them. In the grand scheme of things, we really aren't here very long so I'm going to do everything I can to enjoy it. Limited time, so go for it!

BACK TO CYPRUS

I love my time on holiday but I've noticed my senses have become more heightened. When I was a young girl, six or seven years old, everything was heightened to the point where everything in my life, I found frightening. Every new experience made me feel unsafe.

At school you might have a random music lesson, that would equal change and fear instead of excitement and fun. Nobody knew how I was feeling because I chose to conform and couldn't bear the thought of being singled out. The thought of having to answer a question or God forbid my worst fear, read aloud would feel my whole tiny body with dread, fear and heart palpitations.

It would be fair to say the school environment was a daily nightmare of continual anxiety and misery. I always felt inferior and never up to the educational standard so I would blend in, always conform and present my work beautifully to ensure I wouldn't get noticed.

In fact, I was so well behaved and quiet nobody even bothered to notice I could hardly read by the age of 7. It was by mistake my father one day got me to read aloud and then discovered I basically couldn't. The school was contacted and all of a sudden, I was taught to read which sounds good but it came with a price.

Oh yes, each day I would be singled out to sit with an

often patronising adult who would look at me with pity as though I was a little slow. I overheard one day, one of the teachers discussing me privately with a fellow teacher that all they needed to do was get me to a certain level, but not to worry too much about it for not every child is academic and can amount to much. This hurt, I believed them, I was officially, in the eyes of the world, wait for it, "a thicky!"

So now I was officially one of the thick kids, bloody great! My mind was sharp, I was bright but the fear of learning new maths equations and grammar just sent me in such a spiral of self-doubt, I would simply shut down. Now knowing I was a thicky!

The heart palpitations in class became worse because the thought of being asked to read aloud made me feel physically sick. The anxiety, although very well hidden, had now become a perpetual cycle. If any teachers are reading this book, please if you are going to label a child at such a young age, for goodness sake, don't let them hear you, for a young child will believe you. Oh yes, and most of the time you really do get it wrong!

So back to Cyprus, I've reverted to the fear of my 7-year-old self. I'm bloody 48, I reminded myself to get a grip. Although I'm finding it amusing and very interesting, I'm not enjoying it. At night, I also feel more on edge just like my younger self. Usually, I go to bed and I wonder if anything interesting will happen tonight, but now I feel a childlike fear.

I'm feeling heightened energy in the apartment, but know there is nothing wrong in the apartment like trapped energy. It is my heightened energy creating it. Although I also feel a looming change which I'm resisting.

I decided to make a conscious decision just to go with it because I have learnt these feelings are usually some form of progressing forwards. I have come a long way, previously, I would become absorbed in the situation.

Through experience I have learnt the ability to step out of the moment and watch, analyse and not to forget to ask what is going on. It really is so much easier when you have the ability to ask and be given the truth. Before I share the answer to this, I must let you know what prompted me to ask.

It's dark, I'm restless lying in bed and can't seem to shut down. Instead of getting frustrated, I decided to use the opportunity to go into a meditative state so at least I'll silence my mind and know my body and mind can rest.

That is the beauty of learning the skill of meditation. If you can't sleep at least, you know you are allowing your body and mind some much-needed downtime. Finally, without realising it, I drifted off into sleep. I'm woken up by a large dark mass of energy which looks like a shadow but has an outlined form of perhaps a human or some sort of species.

So, I'm now fully awake and looking at this dark mass

and reverted back to grown up Jane and asked it to show me its real appearance. I'm not in the slightest bit scared for I feel no threat or untoward concern. In the same token, I can't lie and say it feels angelic or uplifting, but it has a strong purpose being there. I asked again to see its true form, but I refused and told firmly to go with it.

You have to understand before I continue, I have the strongest and most protective team who only work in love and light around me. I decided this is a time to just go for it, as I also know I'm given nothing in this life I cannot handle or won't gain or learn from.

That's just how it works for me and until I am proven different, I will TRUST! So, I relax and simply go with it. My jaw starts to have a mind of its own and is moved into end range positions where I must admit I become a little concerned as the jaw is being cracked and lifted out of position making horrendous noises which feels like the noises are ricocheting around my skull.

My head is moved up elevating my shoulders and my head and neck are twisted in positions I thought weren't humanly impossible. All the time, I'm trying to remain in a relaxed state to allow the process to continue. This is not a time to fight it for I'm fully aware I could actually endanger my health and more importantly, my spinal cord.

This episode seems relentless, it goes on and on and I'm

exhausted. My jaw is physically fatigued and my body is aching from all the muscles being activated to elevate my upper body.

Finally it finishes, I lay there thinking, what the hell! Please let this be the end of it for I'm so tired of all these strange, weird and frankly disturbing processes. As you can imagine this was the catalyst to ask my guides what and why is this happening.

What I'm about to show you is one of my writings which was private until I was just given permission to share.

14 Aug 2021, 20.04hrs Cyprus time

Why do I feel such fear and strangely on edge like my 7-year-old self?

The reason for this Jane, is merely change

You are changing rapidly and your senses don't like it

It feels foreign

Rapid change is usually received with resistance

Everything about this process you naturally, mentally and physiologically want to resist

But the process is in motion

Know you are safe and protected

PROTECTED, JANE, PROTECTED!

Do you know what this means?

NO HARM CAN COME YOUR WAY!

Accept the feelings and go with it

Childish behaviour and old behaviour patterns will rear their heads

But

There is no turning back

You are on your way to full recovery

Stronger and more powerful each day

The connection between our two worlds

Are almost completely reunited

Any questions, help, or desires will be fulfilled

So ask wisely and with only good intention and love in your heart

As we know you will.

Do not succumb to fear for fear is a man-made illusion

Illusion, Jane!

Perhaps this is your illusion?

Not for you to over-analyse

For we have no time for this

Philip pops into your head, time and time again

Why is this?

You already know, he is part of the story

Wait and see how the higher intelligent plays with the different scenarios

A challenge will shortly come your way

You will accept and be more than capable

Don't question, just do it!

You are protected at all times

We feel your apprehension as do you

One step at a time

Keep repeating words of trust and positivity

None of the future is your concern

For we have already engineered the outcome.

The world is going to LOVE YOU

Your honesty, simplicity and you

You! For simply being you.

Calmness has already been put upon you

Next is inner courage and strength

You will calmly agree to things you couldn't possibly imagine.

What is it they say?

Dare to be! Dare to be you!

Improvement is rapid

You have already felt and witnessed the process

You will not be asked to do anything

You are not well enough to do.

Don't question, trust, Jane

It has already been engineered

Don't waste time over analysing

This is a process within

Process that will be completed shortly

Shortly

Sooner than you think.

As I have said before in my first book, I have been shown my future. This writing confirms perhaps I am still on track but I'm not hundred percent convinced until I see it for myself. You, as the reader, will know the outcome perhaps in the future for as I have previously said, no way am I releasing this next book unless the first one has helped others.

I have a dream to put something good back into the world before I return home. I still don't know what that is, I have an idea of my own but also know I will be shown exactly what I need to do. So, is all of the above a load of rubbish? Both you and me will have to wait and see!

I'M A LUCID DREAMER

What is a lucid dreamer? In my simple words, a lucid dream is a dream that is so real it feels as real as everyday living. You are literally living, breathing, sensing and feeling every aspect of the dream. I have been told I need to share this dream with you but also the repercussions of how it affected two loved ones in the physical world around me. Make what you wish of the details.

Before I begin, I need to mention I lucid dream a lot to the point I would actually like on occasion to be one of those people who sleep and remember nothing and wake up refreshed knowing you have had a good night's sleep.

This is the dream my spirit guides wanted me to share with you. I'm in the military dressed in green, camouflage combat uniform, the sirens go off and I need to get my military kit ready to deploy. There is always something missing from my kit that puts me on edge. I grab my kit and rush outside.

There are hundreds of soldiers, rushing around on high alert, mayhem everywhere. Soldiers being taken out, shot and killed by hidden snipers, others blown up. There is blood and bodies lying everywhere. The stench in the air is vile.

My adrenaline is so heightened I can physically feel my

heart racing, I have no time for compassion for survival is of greater importance. How I escape the disruption, I don't know, but I have to stay alive. I also have a strong knowing that I'm protected.

It is in the best interest of an intelligent organisation that I must remain unharmed. I'm desperate to escape so I hide behind a building and see a vehicle in the distance, a dark green, military Land Rover. The high pitch, relentless air-raid sirens indicate to everyone there has been a break out of soldiers trying to escape.

The alert state has increased to red. Escapees must be hunted down and killed if they refuse to surrender. The soldiers are all trying to escape for they know they are being scientifically experimented on. Death is a better option than to be manipulated for evil warfare. It literally is survival of the fittest. I see other soldiers patrolling the area in search of the escaped laboratory soldiers.

I managed to get to a dark green military vehicle and opened the door, crouched down and slid into the jeep. Just before I turn the ignition I look into the mirror and stare directly into my eyes. I know one hundred percent it is me, yet I am staring into the face of a scientifically and perfectly engineered species with striking blue eyes, blond hair, perfectly modified features and male. I am strong, powerful and I'm genetically, physiologically perfect.

The one thing that hasn't been completed yet to scientific perfection, is my mind for I know what I am designed to be used for and that is not only evil but corrupt. I stare at myself knowing this is not how I should look but also, I know this is me.

The patrolling soldiers are getting nearer just before I turn the key to the jeep, all of a sudden the connection of the dream is broken and I return to reality. I wake up able to recall the whole dream and find myself hurrying downstairs to frantically write down what I have just witnessed in great detail.

What is going on? I have on other occasions dreamt of being in the military and it always has the same theme, I need to escape the perils of dark, evil engineered corruption and warfare. I have this deep understanding that this dream is very real, perhaps in another time or dimension, but as much as I want to console myself with the fact all of this is made up nonsense and just my imagination, every ounce in my body is screaming this is true!

My dreams can often be extreme but thank goodness, most of the time they don't affect anyone other than myself which I'm very pleased to say. But as you might have already discovered, there is always something lurking around me that can't be explained.

Thankfully what I am about to try and describe is a rarity although I do question the importance of me sharing this information as I have been told there will be others that can also identify with these occurring dreams.

HERE WE GO AGAIN, ANOTHER LUCID DREAM OR PERHAPS, REALITY?

We are on a lovely good old fashioned British holiday in a caravan by the sea. It's overcrowded with a family of five and a dog, so we all have to shuffle who is sleeping where. I'm sharing the double bed with one of my daughters as we can't have a teenager sleeping all day in the sitting room. Lottie, our dog, I am very proud to say is perfectly crate trained so the caravan owners very kindly agree we can bring her.

The night begins with me tossing and turning in bed as I feel strangely on edge and unsettled. I have a knowing that tonight doesn't feel right and I feel a little afraid. I don't breathe a word about how I'm feeling because I certainly don't want to freak out a teenage girl next to me.

My daughter tells me it feels spooky and she is also struggling to sleep. I put this down to the fact she is probably just picking up my energy. We lie in bed and have a little chat as we hear several helicopters fly by which sound familiar, like chinooks. Being from a military background you tend to recognise the difference, generally they are a lot noisier.

Anyway, the night is long for I'm really struggling to sleep but eventually I drift off. I'm back in what feels like a hostile environment. I'm in a brilliant white laboratory, it is spotlessly clean and I can smell a detergent substance lingering in the air.

The smell isn't natural. I can only describe it as some sort of sterile disinfection, but I also have a knowing it isn't. I shouldn't be in this facility but have been deployed to gather intelligence for who? I don't know. I am being used for some sort of matrix higher intelligence. I'm being instructed and used to use the skills I have to gather data which I seem to be compliant with.

That is until I come across a hidden white room with billions of test tubes full of a blue liquid substance which I immediately know is dangerous and threatening to mankind. What I have seen not only could wipe out mankind but has now compromised the safety of the mission and my life. I hear helicopters above my head and instinctively know I must escape with this information.

The intel I have seen is pure evil. My life is now endangered for I can't unsee what I have witnessed and know I can't agree to continue working for this organisation any longer. At this point I wake up lying in bed feeling overwhelmed, horrified and disturbed with what I have witnessed. Is this dream from the past or is this the future?

I have this dreaded pitted feeling in my stomach. I hear

helicopters flying above the caravan and hear in the room crystal clear, the words KILL! KILL! KILL! As I'm lying in bed fully awake, removed from the dream, I see in my mind's eye the billions of blue gel substances in the test tubes being destroyed by military aircraft. I won't lie, I'm petrified; at the same time my daughter wakes up screaming and the dog is going bizarre in the crate barking and scratching at the metal.

First, I calm my daughter down reassuring her there is nothing wrong and then get Lottie out of her crate who is now refusing to get back in it and is shaking uncontrollably. I'm very relieved to be back fully in the materialistic world even though I have two freaked out and extremely frightened members of my family awake.

My daughter reiterates there is something strange going on tonight and she doesn't like it. Lottie won't go back in the crate. I'm too tired to fight with her so we put Lottie on the bed and before long the pair are fast asleep.

I can't sleep for the vivid dream has really upset me and now I have all sorts of questions running through my head. What is real? I decide under no circumstances will I be used to participate in any more warfare games.

I'm not sure how I'm going to do this, but I also know from all my previous dreams nobody has full control over me, I will be protected and finally in this lifetime, break free. I often wonder how much of this journey is real, how much do we create and if there is a higher intelligence controlling the script. I then decide very quickly you could literally blow your mind with what ifs.

I decide quickly to put these thoughts into a box and just get on with this lifetime. I'm told repetitively not to over analyse things by my guides and just write so I decide that's what I'm going to do. I used to wonder why I was privileged to see all these occurrences.

To be quite frank at times, I really would rather not, but then it's not difficult to work it out. It is purely to share with you the reader and finally wake up those who have been happily asleep to perhaps start thinking outside the box. WHO KNOWS? Apparently, all will become evident in time.

This lucid dream or whatever it really is called had a profound effect on me and really upset my creative mind. How I could have been used in any way, shape, or form perhaps in a past or future life for darkness. I needed to speak to my good friend, Becky to make sense of what I had experienced.

Becky is so well read, yes and very sound of mind, the professor of knowledge on all extra crazy, paranormal, alien and unexplainable happenings. If Becky hasn't read a book or got a friend who can explain it, then it's really not worth knowing.

A CONVERSATION I WOULD RATHER HAVE NOT HAD

When I return from my caravan holiday, I'm desperate for a sound mind to put my disturbing dream behind me. "Right Becky, what I'm about to tell you is so ridiculous I think even you might question my sanity," I said. "Lovely! The weirder the better. I'm intrigued," Becky answered.

I'm not always convinced by Becky's explanations, but I'm grateful I have someone who I trust and more importantly, will be blatantly honest with me whether I want to hear it or not. So, in great detail I tell Becky the whole disturbing dream which as I repeat it, I discover it has upset me more than I originally thought. Becky just listens intently and doesn't say a word.

At the end Becky says, "Jane, when you were in the military were there times when you would drift off for periods of time and think that was strange?" I replied yes but then doesn't everyone? Becky asked me a list of other questions which I'm advised not to share with you by my guides. I answered all the questions honestly and had experienced many of them.

Becky was not in the slightest shocked by my dream and the occurrences for she had previously encountered others who had been experiencing almost like flashbacks from their past. Becky then hesitantly said,

"I've always thought you were a super soldier with the things you have described throughout our friendship, but have never said anything for you weren't in the right place to accept this information.

Jane, a super soldier is usually a person from a military background who has special gifts and can be used on a dimensional/spiritual level to access things that others can't. A lot of people who have been used in this way, as they become more awakened start to have flashbacks and dreams on what they have previously done.

This I know will upset you but on a positive note, the more awake you become the more control you have and can no longer through your own choice be used." "F . king hell, Becky! That is sick! I need time to process this, that is horrendous," I told her. "Sorry, Jane, but I feel it's the right time for you to know, there are lots of so-called super soldiers out there and they have even put their lives at risk by speaking the truth."

This new information for the next couple of weeks really brought me down and I became I won't lie, very low. I felt disgusted that I could be used in any other way than pure good. This made me question humanity and more importantly, what I could do about this situation. After a lot of soul searching, I came up with my own conclusion.

Firstly, Becky could have got this one completely wrong.

Secondly, I had noticed I was starting to naturally have an input into my dreams. By this, I mean being able to control them. Thirdly, if there was a possibility I had in any way been used for any other way other than good, truth, honesty and love then I had a lot of making up to do.

I could spend this lifetime getting upset on something that potentially could be a load of bollocks or fight back. I would never be used for anything other than light and that was my right! I felt anger, passion, and determination literally light up inside.

I decided it was Becky's job to know and study all the weird, wonderful and let's face it, often very disturbing other things going on in this world, that so many are oblivious to, which I must mention I think is probably healthy.

Shortly after this conversation, I was severely told off by my guides and told not to over analyse what I had heard and that Becky was on a different path to me. I was not to become consumed in her path and concentrate on my own journey. I was always protected, including my loved ones and that all was required of me at the moment was to write.

I made the decision to focus on my path, write and allow my guides to lead me for I knew in my heart there was a bigger picture to the plan and one full of love. The conversations with Becky are truly fascinating, but I haven't got time to become absorbed nor do I wish to as much as they are intriguing. I need more evidence to be convinced. I had learnt a valuable lesson; we are not always prepared for the truth, however strong we think we are, but we have a choice with what we do and how we behave in the future. Interesting though!

BACK TO CYPRUS - HISTORY PARKS

Whilst we were on holiday in Cyprus much to the kid's horror, we decided it would be a great idea to visit some of the Archaeological history parks. Cyprus is steeped in a wealth of historic knowledge and mystery. We decided to visit two places, the first being the Tomb of the Kings in Paphos.

This is where basically the rich people and their family members were buried. As we walked around, my throat would restrict letting me know there were still spiritual presences remaining but nothing alarming. I had no inclination to investigate because the energy felt pleasant and nonthreatening.

I need to explain, spirit work with mediums in different ways but with me, they first activate my throat that feels like it is being gently squeezed which immediately lets me know spirits are present. It is always my choice whether I choose to open up and communicate with them. If and when I decide to work with spirit, I then receive a mixture of information predominantly by seeing, knowing, sensing, feeling and occasionally hearing.

If there is any danger lurking, the sensation in my throat will be very strong and intense. In the early days of my development, I would feel fearful of these sensations and immediately want to get the hell out of the environment, but now I'm more accepting of shall we say, old energy. I'm respectful of certain historic areas and under no circumstance is this a place to start opening yourself up to have a look at what is really going on.

Years of working with some of the most dedicated and gifted mediums has taught me the art of discipline. I am in control of when and where I choose to use my gifts. Professional mediums do not walk around open to every energy as you would literally be exhausted. On rare occasions, your spiritual team will step in if it's very important.

For example, to prevent a person doing or saying something potentially dangerous, but otherwise you must remain disciplined. Your guides will also let you know instantly if you are in a place riddled with evil, dark and often dangerous energy and yes they do exist! Trust me, if it's dark, evil and strong, every fibre in your body will scream at you to run.

I don't usually gravitate towards old historic buildings, especially churches. We are all led to believe these places are supposed to be angelic, but often they are anything but. My first true encounter of this was when one year we went on holiday to France with my parents and my eldest child.

My father loves anything to do with history where I've never been overly interested. Anyway, the holiday was for all of us so that meant we would spend the day at this beautiful picturesque historic town surrounded by the walls of a castle. My father thought it was amazing, telling us all about the history and I thought it was rather pretty and the shops weren't too bad.

Gosh, I sound ignorant; may I mention as I have got older I'm now starting to become like my parents and quite enjoy history. I think it just eventually comes with age! Anyway, my father is desperate to go into this little old church at the end of the island.

I feel immediately on edge, I don't want to, but I have a strong word with myself and reiterate, for goodness sakes Jane, it's just a church and it doesn't even look like it will take long to get around from the outside. It looks small and pretty insignificant.

As soon as I step in, it fills my body with dread and horror. Get a grip Jane! As I walk further into the church, it feels dense, the smell resembles death, a distinct smell of human flesh. Every ounce of my body says to run straight back out of the door.

The military training kicks in, no pain, no gain, do it! I walk around, now the darkness and evil of this presence best described as a large smog of heavy, dense black treacle substance expanding and trying to engulf me. Its presence I can see is everywhere within the church, yet it is drawing closer towards me as though intrigued by my presence.

I feel and hear screaming and crying echoing from the walls. In my mind's eye, I see blood seeping from the walls. Enough is enough! I must get out, I can't breathe. Sorry, Dad, I've got to get out. Finally, I'm in the fresh air, I feel nauseous, unclean and very disturbed by the horror of being in a house of prayer! What the hell has just happened?

I can't make sense of the turmoil and evil I have just felt. I decided to confide in my dad and tell him how awful being in that church was." Yes, that would make sense, so much evil went on in those times. I'm not surprised, Jane, it was really rather barbaric how the people were treated," said my Dad.

I then got another history lesson which I really needed to know before I agreed to step into that frighteningly evil, unassuming, sweet little church. With time and experience, you learn your limits.

Most historic places have a certain amount of energy still present which is fine and the majority of churches are situated on grid lines which I know very little about, but always heighten my sensitivity to the energy around and course a tight restriction in my throat.

Again, at first this used to scare me but with knowledge and a knowing that you are always in control, it really isn't a problem. But in the same token, if the energy feels like the little church in France, I will always choose to step away.

Some things in life we haven't got explanations for and who knows maybe never will, but that doesn't make it untrue and incredibly dangerous. I will always choose light over darkness.

I'm just so thankful I have been chosen in the future to work with light not dark for some as in my previous book Michael didn't always get a choice. Michael will be explained in more detail, later in the book.

Now, I don't want you all thinking churches are unholy places. I have to admit they are not my favourite place to frequent but on that note, I must tell you about a church I visited in Greece which has been one of my most humbling and uplifting experiences.

Prior to having kids, Tony and I would go on lots of cheap budget holidays abroad, our favourite place to visit was Greece. The reason I love it so much is because the places we visited were simply breathtaking, beautiful, rural and made you appreciate nature and the simple things in life.

We would stay in basic, clean accommodation with no extra luxuries as at the time we were both on low wages.

We would always splash out and either hire a car or go on a coach trip to explore the island. We were always drawn to the older parts of Greece for we weren't interested in the build-up areas with nightclubs and overly commercialised parts.

We wanted to see how the locals lived, the food they ate and the places they would respect and frequent. One of the days we visited an older part of one of the towns and we visited a church, it felt fine and was highly respected by everyone.

We walked around and paid our respects, but as we walked around, I couldn't help noticing the wealth, opulence and gold literally hanging off the walls.

This I am assured was to show respect for just how important God's house of worship is. The local people throughout history would offer whatever little means they had to the church, which for many was very little.

Literally as soon as you stood outside the church, what struck me was even today the locals lived very basic and simple lives. It was like two different worlds! I can't and still to this day don't understand why churches are full of such wealth when surely the leaders of faith know it means nothing on the other side.

I learnt from my catholic upbringing that Jesus was born into very humble beginnings with very little and left with nothing.

So why do churches still today consist of such opulence when so many go hungry and die of disease? (Just an observation, I have no intention of offending anyone!)

Anyway, whilst we explored this town we were told by a local, about a very well known healer and you could visit this church where apparently he used to heal people. Now that sounds much more my cup of tea, Tony wasn't so enthralled, but I managed to persuade him.

When we finally got to the place, it was basically this tiny little church in the middle of an unkempt land with a rugged, dry and dusty off-road path. Just before the tiny, shed sized church was a restaurant ideal for any passing tourists and that was literally it.

I had to stop myself from laughing as the disappointment of travelling so far to see this tourist attraction was written across Tony's face. "Well, we are here now so let's take a look," I said trying to lift the mood.

As we arrived, several people were leaving so by the time we got to step inside, it was empty. The church was tiny with very few wooden pews, a stone basin at the front and little else apart from a picture of what we presumed must have been the healer.

There was nothing to explore, no gold dripping from the walls, just a humble house of prayer. I felt emotional because it felt so humble and pure. A calmness, inner peace, safety and acceptance washed over me that almost reduced me to tears. I didn't want to leave. As Tony decided to leave, I told him I just wanted to stay a little longer.

I found myself in this church on my own fixated on the

painting of this dark haired, handsome looking man. I just stood in a dazed state staring into his eyes which had now become real. His eyes were a deep dark brown, strong, but also gentle. In this present moment, our worlds had emerged as one.

I was in a state of trance fixated by this powerful, healing and humbling presence. I could see a light surrounding his head as our two worlds became one. I suddenly became startled as I could hear someone approaching.

What had just occurred? Why had it occurred? Was it real or a figment of my imagination? I don't know what just happened, but it felt good, right, pure and beautifully loving. All this loving energy from a tiny insignificant church not much bigger than a large shed in the middle of nowhere.

I don't question that lots of healing miracles took place in that tiny church. I have a deep inward knowing that not only was this man a gifted healer, but he was honourable, humble and an exceptionally kind and loving man.

Apparently, people in the past would travel miles with their sick loved ones to be healed by this man. What I loved so much about the story of this healer was he had very little, gave everything he had to help others and was a true lightworker.

The real deal! I have a strong feeling that is what God,

the loving divine, whatever you want to call it, if you choose to believe, would have wanted. I wonder if the above is disappointed at how man has interpreted his legacy.

AGAIN BACK TO CYPRUS

I digress: the second historic site we visited was on the harbour of Paphos. Fascinating, well worth a visit, oh gosh, I'm turning into my parents, yikes! It's August, the strength of the sun is unbearable and the air is stifling, but I keep being drawn to certain locations.

I find myself standing in barren locations that aren't for the tourists fixated on just feeling the strength of the ground and seeing the dedication and discipline of men perfecting their weapon skills for survival. I feel my whole body tingle with euphoria.

I feel powerful and strong. I don't want to leave as the sensation of courage is like nothing I have ever experienced before. I'm literally standing there with no one around as my family has already grown tired of being in the blazing heat outside and have taken shelter.

Tony always has the ability to know when I need a strange, quiet moment. There are no tourists around just me, feet glued to the earth and I hear and feel the wind upon my face as though surrounding me with strength and courage. For that moment in time, time stood still, there was no one else but me and courage.

I could have bathed in the sensation longer but the scorching sun is relentless and the kids need feeding. Just as we were about to leave, I had this overbearing sensation that I had to visit another location. This time, a building with artefacts.

The bored kids decided to remain in the shelter as I kept apologising to Tony for having to go back. Whilst inside the building I was immediately drawn to a mosaic of a person on an eagle, instantly symbolising freedom!

I felt overwhelmed with a deep knowing my time was coming and I would feel freedom. How, when, where, who knows but it was coming!

I have previously seen and been offered from one of my spirit guides, three feathers. I have received two, calmness and strength/courage, but still wait for the final feather which will be peace!

This will enable me to finally be free from perhaps I sometimes wonder, the obstacles and burdens I have chosen to carry maybe from previous lives or just this life. Anyway, two out of three isn't bad, I'm looking forward to peace!

CONTROLLING DREAMS, IS THIS A REALITY?

Whilst in Cyprus, I'm dreaming loads, but I've noticed a huge change. I'm saying no and taking control of what is happening in my other life, the life of dreams!

The dream begins with me driving in Australia, the weather is beautiful, I have my Mum sitting next to me as a passenger. We are chatting away admiring the beautiful, picturesque mountains full of an array of different shades of green, beautiful tropical flowers and ripened fruit, it really is breathtaking.

I feel so happy, content and loving life. More importantly, I'm with a person I can really have a good laugh with, feel safe, loved and free to be one hundred percent myself, my gorgeous Mum! We continue driving through the mountains and then drive through a town heading towards the beach.

As we drive around the next corner, we are startled by the sun's reflection of a spectacular crystal clear, light blue sea. We decide not to stop for the ocean's waves are huge and the situation feels strangely threatening and unpredictable.

As much as the water looks inviting, we both decide to carry on driving to find somewhere to grab a coffee.

The scenario changes again, the landscape has become

flatter as though we are driving through farming land. On the left is a beautiful large, calm and mesmerising lake. We both agree that this would be a nice place to find somewhere to grab a drink.

Straight ahead, we see two men standing on the side of the road, so we decide to ask them if there is a nearby coffee shop. The men are friendly, warm and bizarrely, familiar. We are all chatting away having a giggle when suddenly, the car in front disappears into a sinkhole.

The ground has completely collapsed and the huge hole has quickly filled with murky brown water. The suction of the car plunging into the depths of darkness causes one of the men to fall in. Our car is less than a metre away from the gaping hole as I scream at my mum to get back and away from the water as I know this is incredibly dangerous as she can't swim.

I'm torn between helping the other man and keeping my Mum safely away from this awful situation. I go to help the man as my mum has safely moved away. I turn my back for a split second and my mum has jumped into the murky, filthy, brown sinkhole to rescue the man who earlier fell in.

I'm standing frozen staring over a large hole which is surreal, the water is calm with no sign of life. I feel heartbroken, physically sick and in great despair. I start to gag as the heartache is unbearable. "NO!" I will not allow this to happen, I jump into the hole knowing full well the dangers and the risk I am taking, but will not allow this tragic loss of life without a fight.

I feel the cold water against the whole of my body as I plunge deeper and deeper into the dark, cloudy brown water. I can't see anything, I have no sense of direction and feel disorientated, but decide to go deeper. I'm now struggling for breath as I have literally no oxygen left in my lungs and my chest physically hurts. I feel something, I grab desperately at what I presume is an arm.

The lack of oxygen and the weakness within my body is starting to drag me down in the depths of the darkness. "NO!" with my last chance of survival should I let go of this person? "NO!" I feel a burst of energy just before I reach the surface and take a large gasp of air. It's my Mum, I can feel her weak heart beating against my hand, her heart is in my hand.

She is lifeless, her eyes are wide open, but I notice her pupils are large and black, the life in front of me is fading away. I feel panic, I don't know what to do as there is no one to help me get myself and my mum out of this hole.

I try breathing into her mouth without succeeding and then I decide frantically to breathe repeatedly into her face, why I don't know, I just can't give up. I will not give up! I can't give up! My mum's eyes suddenly start to react to the light and return to normal. My mum starts to sputter, she is back in the land of the living.

I wake up from the dream so upset with the same pitted feeling and anxiety in my stomach. What was all of that about, how traumatic!

For the rest of the day, I keep getting flashbacks of my Mum's lifeless black eyes. I ask my guides why do you allow these dreams to be so vivid? What is the purpose? I'm told the purpose is to start taking control, I have always had the ability, but the time is right, now. You can't be controlled unless you choose to be.

Somewhere and somehow along my journey, I have learnt or chosen to control my dreams. As a child, I would wake up petrified and simply accept the outcome of what I had experienced. I would often spend the day feeling traumatised with what I had felt, sensed, seen and heard.

Feeling awkward and silly, I would never share my dreams for what would the adults in my world think?

I certainly wasn't going to take the risk or be fobbed off with dreams are only dreams, it's all in your imagination. How could my dreams mean nothing when they are as real as the material world?

What are dreams, perhaps another time in another dimension? Who knows, I'm sure the scientists would laugh at my stupidity and perhaps naivety, but as we already know, science is only real once it has been proven. It's a well-known fact neurologists and brain specialists have only discovered such a small percentage of how the brain works.

If specialists really understood the brain surely, they would have worked out a cure for the millions of people suffering from migraines? More importantly, as humans, how much of our brains do we use? The answer is, nobody truly knows.

We can all make educated predictions, but as we have known through history, man often makes mistakes.

So, my point is, are dreams what we are led to believe or do we flitter perhaps through other dimensions. I hear the thoughts of many, crazy woman!

Yes, maybe, only time will tell. I always think it is positive to have an open mind and question everything.

I have another crazy thought, perhaps the bigger plan is for humans to become so absorbed in technology, media and fed what we think we believe to be true that we eventually lose the ability to think for ourselves.

How many people have views on topics they have been drip fed through social media?

How about, how do you feel, what are your views, what do you really believe to be true?

What does your gut instinct tell you? Experiences of your own, making your own memories or even spending time without technology so you can breathe and find out who you are?

Wouldn't it be refreshing if we all decided to return to using our own senses and instincts which are still very much within us? At any time, we have the ability to think, sense and basically reignite our human senses which would enable us to take back control of our journey.

The alternative is to become carried along in this lifetime being told what to think, feel and even behave. When you see the above written in black and white, it's quite frightening and a little alarming.

So much mental ill health, I wonder could this have anything to do with the fast pace of life when secretly we all crave the basics? The basics of being in another's presence, a hug, fresh air, greenery and so important trees?

Time to stop, stand still and feel the wind upon your face. When was the last time you remember acknowledging the sensation and elements of the weather and really feeling it?

The simplicity of nature is so powerful it allows people even if just for a short while to calm and silence the busy mind which is unfortunately, often consumed with perpetual thoughts of what one must do or even worse self-sabotaging with self-doubt and a lack of self-worth or belief.

If there is only one word of advice, I can truly speak from my heart, that is, please all of you get into nature, or even just watch the birds from your window, which will allow you escapism from this busy world.

The mind, body and spirit will be energised and given a well deserved break which will make you feel happier.

I'm on a roll now! As for our children, get them off their gadgets. Yes, it will probably cause an argument, but this really is important for their mental well-being.

Take them for a walk. It's amazing what you will find out from the conversation and actually what is going on with their life. You might be surprised to hear they are struggling with school, friendship issues or feeling perhaps fearful of this busy world, being fed negativity from every angle of social media.

Childhood and adolescence can be a really difficult time. I can't say I have met loads of people who loved school. Imagine how stressful it must feel living through a pandemic as well.

You will never know the truth of what is going on inside a child's mind unless you spend time with them. If a kid, as I know, has a choice of going on a walk or playing on a gadget, they will pick the latter. What is it they say with kids, especially teenagers, pick your fights.

Well, this will probably cause a fight, but it will be worth the arguments to give your kids the opportunity with no distractions, the opportunity to express their feelings, fears and find out what is going on in their world.

As adults, we can choose to rush around and implode, but we at least need to teach our kids the value of nature and taking time out.

BACK TO CYPRUS IN THE REAL WORLD?

I love being in Cyprus. I have this wonderful feeling of escapism so much so, I actually don't want to go back home. I can genuinely say I love the slower pace of life, the local people and the simplicity of this way of life.

The traffic is minimal, the hustle and bustle significantly reduced and there is this wonderful feeling of space and freedom. I tell Tony if I could, I would leave all my possessions and stay out here.

The reality is I have to go back because the kids need to go back to school and one of my children would miss her friends and social life. Only one out of five of us would miss the rat race but we are a family so we stay as a family.

Tony is amused, as usually after a couple of weeks, I'm usually thankful to go back home but not this time. I try to explain that back home everyone seems to be rushing around, congregating in the same huge impersonal shopping venues and leisure facilities.

Smaller independent shops are struggling to survive and many unfortunately are being forced to close. Local small and personal hospitals no longer exist due to creating larger facilities we can all herd into.

The personal local village school is being built to expand

for the increasing number of people moving into new housing in the area. STOP!

Where is the community and personal care of knowing one another? It's still there, but now you really have to search for it. If I am completely truthful, I have this feeling of impending change and suppression again.

I don't know yet what it is, but it's imminent. I also feel no regret, yet I do feel apprehension about releasing that bloody book! So, it would be easier to run away, bury my head in the sand and stay out here.

The final day of the holiday has arrived, I feel sad and anxious. The natural ability to breathe in the sea air, hear the crash of the waves upon the shore and absorb every aspect of nature is drawing to an end. I choose to detach myself from the emotion and resort to the old military Jane who goes into autopilot.

Emotions put into a box, now time to get on with the task ahead, back to reality. The military is quite unique as it teaches you to compartmentalise all aspects of your life. The longer you stay in this environment, the easier it is to move to a new area, build friendships, leave and move on.

I still can't work out if this is a good or bad thing. I suppose there are equally positives and negatives.

The only thing I do question is, over time, if you learn to detach too much and lose the ability to show vulnerability and expression of your feelings due to fear of ridicule or looking weak, this will inevitably take a toll on your health.

Perhaps another reason so many ex-military personnel live with hidden mental ill-health and suffer in silence. (Just a thought!)

BACK HOME

Within a few days of returning home, our holiday becomes a distant memory. It's time to get back on the wheel of fitting into society. That wonderful time of year when parents are rushing around trying to get new school shoes and uniforms all crammed into overcrowded shopping centres.

The atmosphere always feels of heightened stress and anxiety as parents rush to complete their final jobs before returning their sweet and delightful children back into formal institutes. (Deep joy!)

For a moment, I sound quite normal so once again, I shall burst that bubble. I finally have the house to myself and decide I'm going to meditate.

I sit in silence and before long I feel the presence of several beings. It's familiar, strangely comforting and I feel one hundred percent safe, so simply bathe in the energy.

I've also noticed the intensity feels powerful, but not only that it feels purer, clear, closer and easier to be in.

As I lie there, my jaw is gently being moved in very precise movements and it feels rather pleasant. I can honestly say I'm shocked by that last statement, but it's true. I'm quite enjoying the subtlety of the gentle moves.

In fact, it's quite mesmerising and extremely relaxing. All of a sudden, I feel the same familiar surgical metal cold device being inserted into my mouth which I have experienced before.

This time, the device fits perfectly and doesn't pinch the flap of skin underneath my tongue. The best way to describe this once again is as the same sensation as when the dentist puts that awful appliance in your mouth under your tongue before taking an X-ray.

I'm lying there not bothered and have got to a stage where the stranger, almost the better. Anyway, the device feels comfortable as though it has been adjusted to fit my mouth, it's bearable so I just go with it. All of a sudden, something was physically moved inside my mouth under my tongue to the left which resulted in my left scapular, shoulder blade being popped and released.

I reluctantly must admit I also felt something being released under my tongue that slivered down my throat and into my spine. Yikes! Surely, physiologically, this couldn't be possible.

So, the next time I have a chiropractor appointment, I'm desperate to know if this could be physically possible.

How do I find out without sounding ridiculous? I have an inquisitive mind and just need to know. At the end of the chiropractor treatment, I word my question with caution and make out I'm just so fascinated by anatomy

117

and physiology that could the manipulation of the tongue release pressure and muscles of the scapular?

I'm confident she will look at me with a questioning and amusing expression, but no! She replies that there are practitioners who specialise in working inside the mouth including moving the tongue to relief muscles/fascia throughout the body.

So why have I never met one, maybe I could be further down the line now.

The chiropractor also mentioned how pleased she was with the improvement in my neck. (I have to admit I didn't mention the strange sensation of something slithering under my tongue down my throat into my spine.

Some things are definitely better off not mentioning!) I then come to a realisation that I genuinely don't think or believe that what I have so far experienced is humanly possible.

If humans had evolved these advanced techniques we wouldn't still have people spending all their hard earned money searching for cures to relieve their pain.

Lightbulb moment! I must wait for the procedure to be finished. I've always known this, but I've just been too desperate to move through this chapter quicker. Whilst sat in front of my computer I am told.

"Jane, you have to wait until the spirit world has finished the process. (No shit, Sherlock!)

There really is no one who can help you, all of this process is on a timeline, as you will eventually see." I know this to be true, I always have, they have told me enough times, but the problem is I'm not always accepting of things I don't want to hear, especially if I have no clue to when the finishing date of hardships is going to end.

I'm sure all of you can relate to this as I have been told repeatedly this is a human floor. Finally, the penny has dropped. I might not like the outcome, but it's the truth. It doesn't matter how hard I search for a cure, maybe it's time to accept the process for what it is and be thankful I am going to make a full recovery.

There is always something so fulfilling when you accept situations and finally stop fighting. I have this theory that hasn't been proven yet and that is, once you accept the situation for what it is, the wheel of life moves on again to a different stage or chapter.

THE WHEEL MOVES AGAIN

I'm feeling upbeat and more accepting of life. It's like a huge burden has been lifted off my shoulders as I have accepted the process of what will be, will be. Life feels good, I feel positive and every time I feel off balance or poorly, I have this strong sense everything is going to be fine and I'm no longer going to let it worry me.

I have the choice and freedom to respond to any situation in life how I want to and it feels empowering and bloody good to finally go with it. I wish I had discovered this new way of thinking earlier. It would have made this life so much more enjoyable, but at least I finally got there.

I've been having regular massages for the discomfort in my body caused by my younger physical days. It's expensive, but I'd rather keep my body functioning this way than consuming daily painkillers.

I no longer worry about the discomfort in my body from old injuries and have a healthy relationship with the situation knowing that if you acknowledge and connect to pain, you will notice it changes all the time. The more you tense and fight pain, the worse it becomes.

I can't recommend mindfulness for health enough; it really is quite life-changing. I decided to have a go at mindfulness when I was watching a well-known TV show on the discussion of mindfulness. I remember listening to one of the opinionated women sitting on the panel.

Her opinion was she thought it was a load of rubbish, but actually her opinion was floored for she hadn't even tried it.

This woman for some reason really got under my skin to the point I had to find out for myself. We are all entitled to opinions, however I would rather listen to the opinion of a person who has experiences rather than views on what they have read.

That was the catalyst, where I became intrigued to see if this mindfulness had any real substance to it. Within a few days, I was buying a book for a child's birthday and came across a mindfulness book with a free DVD which seemed perfect as it literally talked you through the whole process.

This book explained the science in great detail, no airy fairy explanations, just simply straight talking and factual. I decided I would have a go, it was an eight week programme and I promised myself however boring it became I would complete it.

One of my strengths is if I decide to do something, I will finish it. I won't lie or flower up the situation because at first it was incredibly boring, took time, and discipline. Putting the course into perspective, it only took small, allocated periods of time to do during the day and the results are well worth the effort.

After three weeks of dedicating myself to the course, I thought that opinionated women with no experience on mindfulness could be right, but something inside me thought you still haven't got a valid opinion until you have completed the course.

After four weeks, I felt different, happier and more content. I put this down to the relaxation technique. I genuinely, a strange thing to say, liked myself. I felt happy in my own skin, I can't recall ever feeling like this in my entire life, but it felt good.

I also noticed the discomfort in my body had reduced and I could live alongside it where before it almost consumed me.

Don't get me wrong, it hasn't cured me, but taught me the tools to escape this busy world. The most important thing I learnt was how everything keeps moving and evolving, including physical pain.

The anxiety of what felt at times as the body failing me, by this I mean not always being able to do the things I wanted to do for example walking for hours on end up, strenuous, beautiful mountains was strangely OK!

The fight and disappointment within myself was calmer, more bearable and accepting. I loved this new feeling. It was alright to be me in this chapter of life with no external pressures, more importantly from the harshness of myself.

I identified very quickly that it was me making my health worse, me that was putting pressure on myself to get better quicker.

Finally, I'm disappointed to say it was me who wasn't allowing my body, mind and soul to work out the healing process.

With time, patience, acceptance and most important trust in the spirit world, I would make a full recovery.

By the end of the course, my children had commented on how much more relaxed and happy I seemed. Wait for it! Even my husband commented on how content I was. Let's face it ladies, the fact my husband noticed a change has to prove something was going on and more importantly, it was a positive change.

So do I still use mindfulness?

Initially every day, but as I felt better and better, I became less disciplined but it doesn't matter because I have learnt the tools and know how to reverse my old ways of thinking and quickly become aware if I am creating tension throughout my body, especially the neck and shoulders.

Would I recommend mindfulness?

Definitely for it reduces anxiety, teaches you to relax physically which will help those who struggle with daily physical discomfort, but more importantly, it allows you the freedom and choice to remove yourself from this often hectic life.

Any opportunity to give yourself a break from your thoughts and society even for a few minutes is gold dust. There is only one way to find out if mindfulness will help you and that is not to listen to others' views, but find out for yourself, just don't expect instant results, it takes time.

Most things in life worth having, take time, effort and a desire to improve your life. I've learnt that the majority of changes I want to achieve in this life, often come from yourself and we all have the right to improve our health whether that be physically or mentally.

Professional people can help, but real results come from yourself! (Just my opinion!)

I had no idea I was going to waffle on about mindfulness, but my guides have strongly insisted I share my experience with you, the reader. I have no doubt it will help many of you!

I also have a knowing that by relaxing my mind and body will enable my spiritual team easier access to developing me!

I'VE FOUND ANOTHER HIDDEN HEALER

I'm reluctant to discuss this with you, but have been told I must, that's how writing these last two books works which at times genuinely horrifies me. I must make it clear, if my identity comes out in the future, please don't assume you know the people for I have been treated by many.

I have been having massage treatments regularly and immediately knew this person has the ability to heal.

Whether this person is aware or not, if it's meant to be at some point it will come to light. Also, I don't make a habit of discussing I am a medium as I like to take my time sussing the person out, sometimes often years before having that discussion.

Why? Because I like people to know me as just Jane – not a medium who some will suddenly think you are reading their mind or have all the answers to their problems. I don't want to be someone's personal medium/psychic.

I want to live in the real world and talk about perhaps how challenging the teenage years are, how I'm bored of cooking dinners, house work and juggling life, in general.

I have enough friends I can talk to about mediumship

and psychic topics, but I really value having friends who have no interest or very little knowledge on these subjects. Plus, it keeps this time on earth more real and grounded which I want to live in.

When I return home, another dimension, heaven, whatever it is you want to call it, I want to go back with a wealth of knowledge and experiences. Also, if I'm totally honest, I used to worry what they would think. Most of my friends are fine, usually laugh and say, "Well, I would never have expected that, you are so normal."

I'm not sure whether that is a compliment or not, but it doesn't make any difference to our friendship, perhaps a few questions initially, but then we revert back to how we were before.

I had judged one friend wrong in my early days which was a shame because she just couldn't get her head around it and almost looked a little afraid of me which was sad as I found her good company. Not everyone can accept a person who has the ability to talk to so-called dead people.

I totally get it, especially if they have been brought up in a religious background and I completely respect that is their choice, but I'm still Jane, the same person!

In my younger days, there was no way on earth I was going to reveal my true self. I was unable to accept myself being a medium and I had no desire to speak of it. Surely, if I couldn't accept my true self, society would ridicule and reject me.

If we are being totally honest, nobody likes rejection, so it is much easier to conform to this world and keep quiet.

So sad how so many people hide their true self. I often think the world would be even more colourful and beautiful if people were true to themselves, definitely happier, but again sometimes it inevitably comes with a cost.

I just want to say I'm happy with who I am and don't apologise for what I am able to do because it has helped heal the hearts of many. I'm finally okay with who I am!

That statement has made me really emotional for it has been a gruelling long road. I'm so glad I have been born in these times, society is changing all the time and thank goodness, becoming more open-minded. Back to the hidden healer I am trying to put off writing about.

I arrived for my usual painful, deep tissue massage. The room feels immediately different, almost as though someone has turned up the intensity and heat in the room. I'm greeted by a warm welcome and we have our usual jovial banter about how wonderful life is before we start. The massage is going well, but then I start to feel incredibly hot and feel a very strong presence in the room. I know immediately who it is, but say nothing.

We both remain silent as this time feels of great importance and not for idle chit chat. As I'm being massaged, the pain is heightened to the point it is becoming unbearable, suddenly I notice the familiar character again who always presents himself to me as a native American Indian standing to the right of me, staring into my eyes with his hands crossed upon his chest.

I know this to be one of my guides who is let's say straight to the point, blunt, disciplined and incredibly powerful. Not exactly a laugh a minute, but good at what he can do and whilst working with him in previous situations always produces exceptional results.

His intensity is literally of the scale. He instructs me to keep looking into his eyes and focus. He tells me pain is a man-made illusion, that I am strong and can go through any amount of pain for I have already succeeded in this lifetime.

Bloody hell, I feel nauseous and a little lightheaded for the muscles the masseur has been guided to work on are new and stomach churningly painful. I find myself drifting into my guide's eyes, almost removing myself from the pain and the situation.

I allow my guide in a strange way to absorb the pain! The situation, thank goodness, moves on, this time to around my neck.

As the massage therapist starts to work on my neck, I

notice her hands have changed into an indigenous man's.

I find this fascinating as I'm still very aware my guide is still standing to my right. The movements are so precise, gentle, strong and powerful. There was no doubt in my mind the therapist was in a light trance and her hands were being guided exactly where to go. A technique too advanced for a fellow human, superior and so much more advanced.

The heat radiating from my body was blissful and very calming. I felt completely at ease and in safe hands almost like an inner part of me had surrendered to the process. Whilst this sensation is going on, I'm handed from my guide a white feather as to be rewarded with peace!

I feel emotional, humble and honoured to be allowed to experience such a beautiful experience. The intensity in the room returns to normal as the spirit guides disappear and the massage therapist moves away from me.

We are initially both a little speechless and then I comment, "Well, that was intense! You do realise you were being used for healing?"

The massage therapist opened up that she had been involved in healing before, but that was intense. I also mentioned that her hands had changed to an Indian man's which made her burst out laughing for someone who she loved very dearly always implied she was from Indian descent.

For months, neither of us had ever talked about any form of spiritual awareness, but now we knew we could speak freely in the comfort of one another.

In the future, I knew this massage therapist would only grow more in strength. Some people play with healing, but this person had been handpicked from above and her journey was only to become more magical.

A good healer will have the ability to stop the over analytical mind and trust in the process. This person had no ego, wanted to help people and whether she knew it or not was wise, tribal and gifted.

This person in the future would be aligned with those people who were failed by Western medicine and more importantly, needed her gentle, healing, safe and kind presence.

After that session, I thanked my guides for leading me to another lightworker and perhaps in the future we could help each other, even if that just simply meant being able to talk openly and have a laugh about this beautiful and often unassuming life.

It often seems on my journey when I start to question what the hell I am doing writing my truth and whether it is real or has any benefit or purpose in this lifetime, I'm given another carrot that someone else can confirm I'm not a flaming loony. Hope gets put back on the table and for another period of time, I stay focused and true to myself.

I do question my path and hopefully always will for if I didn't surely, I would become ungrounded and away with the fairies.

For a logically minded person, I do struggle with this spiritual path for I like witnessing and experiencing things for myself and need proof. I have been shown so much and thankfully in a lot of cases with others as witnesses which should make it more real, yet I hunger for more evidence.

I really do question why they didn't pick someone else who would embrace and believe all these experiences with appreciation and acceptance. Don't get me wrong, I have grown to love it, but I want the opportunity to blow the minds of the sceptics.

My gifts are becoming stronger. I don't know where all of this is going although I have my suspicions. I hope in my lifetime someone develops their skills beyond human understanding and blows the minds of all those sceptic scientists. I know this exists, but not to the point where it can't be argued against.

Imagine a lightworker who could heal the sick with no scientific explanation. I can hear the scientist already, "There is not enough scientific evidence!" Maybe not everything in this life can be explained or needs to be understood, but that doesn't make it unreal.

The world is becoming so much more accepting of alternative therapies as people don't always want the side effects of pharmaceutical chemicals that can dull the experience of being here. I see a positive future where there will be more gifted lightworkers able to work naturally and not having to hide behind qualifications to make them more acceptable.

My friend Becky, has done so many different courses on reflexology to life coaching but really, what is she?

She is basically a very talented medium. So, why can't she just own it? Because once again, we want to fit into society without being ridiculed.

I have made a decision once my health and spiritual alignment is completed, I'm going to embrace everything that is thrown at me.

I might not always like it, but I also appreciate that we are here for such a limited time. If reincarnation exists, which from what I have seen I no longer doubt, I don't want to come back in another life and have to learn this journey again! NO, THANK YOU!

I SOUND LIKE A BROKEN RECORD

I've decided not to write about any more strange healing and manipulation occurrences for I've just been told quite rudely I'm sounding like a broken record and have to agree.

Strange and scientifically unexplained events are regularly happening to me which are humbling, loving and to be totally honest at times, a little unnerving.

I asked recently why it needs to take so long for I have witnessed, felt and seen the power of this, let's call it divine energy. I'm simply told my health will improve on a specific timeline and to keep writing. I decide it is much easier to digest if I keep it simple, I know it's loving and pure, so I'm happy to work with it.

I received a writing on 8th of September 2021, which I would really rather not share so I have compromised with my spirit guides and agreed to share the writing if these books are a success. I can tell you, on completion of the first 'The Reluctant Medium,' I was given a specific list of people to send a copy to and shown future events.

I was also told to add the writing in this book, but every ounce in my body disagrees so I'm not going to on this occasion. Yes, I'm being deviant, but I think that's a good thing occasionally if it prevents you from looking too much like an arse! I'll share the writing in the future if these books are successful, but won't reveal other's names.

One of the reasons I've released this next book is to see if my future predictions are true or simply a load of rubbish. I have made a promise with the spirit world that however modified and embarrassed I am to be associated with these books, if they are successful, I will rise to the occasion and own them.

Yikes, that would be tough because I've hidden my truth since birth. I literally feel sick at the prospect of sharing my journey and genuinely feel quite nauseous at the thought of all this becoming a reality. Logic would say, this is surely all a lot of nonsense so carry on Jane writing the truth for nobody will get to see it!

I haven't got time or the strength or desire to think of the alternative. I've also thought of a cunning back up plan, I could admit to these books and then disappear living as a recluse in the forest, hidden out of sight.

See, there is always a positive in every negative if you look hard enough!

MORE VISITORS IN THE NIGHT

Whilst reading this book, you probably think every night I go to sleep I'm visited by spirits from the other side.

This is not true; it tends to be quite extreme and busy with visitors and occurrences and then often it can go quiet for sometimes, a couple of months.

When it goes quiet, the dreams tend to be more heightened. I tend to live a busier life whilst asleep and I've become so familiar with it, I feel a little disappointed if I'm not shown something that I can analyse and question in the material world.

It's like I've become a sponge wanting to understand and witness for myself other dimensions. The intensity and craziness has gradually increased the more I have become accepting and comfortable with it all. It does help knowing and trusting in the strong, protective team around me who have proven time and time again, no harm can come my way for I've been assured there is a purpose to all of this.

The time and dedication that has been invested in me has been constant. My team works around the clock to perfect our connection for future events. Whatever these future events will be, I have made a conscious decision that I will face whatever is thrown my way and get on with it, as it will only be to benefit all in a loving pure way and to open the minds of all.

The funny thing is I spent the first thirty-two years doing everything in my power not to work with spirit. I can honestly say I would feel sad and incomplete without my spiritual team working with me for this life would bore the hell out of me without having these wonderful although often frightening experiences.

I have gone from the persistent feeling of a frightened child to a woman who craves knowledge and understanding. This world, although beautiful, doesn't completely satisfy my soul anymore. Don't get me wrong, I'm happy and thankful for this life, but also know there is so much more to it that I do believe has already been discovered, but hasn't been released for fear of how humans would respond.

I like to think us humans are more accepting than given credit for and would adjust to new knowledge. The truth will eventually come out and all those so-called crazy people who perhaps shared too much of their knowledge will be considered normal!

I as you know have my friend Becky the professor as I call her, who informs me of all crazy paranormal stuff. I listen to her advice and knowledge, but I have to admit some of it is too advanced for me. I don't ridicule or laugh at her information. I just sit on the fence and think that's too advanced and crazy for me, I need further proof. Also, I love a good diverse conversation as it opens my mind in a way otherwise I wouldn't.

I have also been told several times by my spirit team that under no circumstances, I am to become consumed with Becky's knowledge for that is Becky's path and not mine. I am to write, nothing more, nothing less. I am given permission to continue my mediumship work, but the priority is for me to write.

The problem is I'm a bit like a child in a sweet shop and I want to do it all. I want to do readings for others. I like the sense of fear whilst standing up in front of people with no information and having to trust and connect with spirit and prove the survival of death.

As much as I dread the fear, I crave it! But I have also learnt from my past, if you don't listen, you will crash and burn. I have witnessed some of the most talented mediums suffer horrific illnesses, unable to walk without walking devices and even one suffered an unknown health episode similar to a stroke.

She was young and probably the most gifted medium I have had the honour of seeing work. She channelled drawings from her non-writing hand and they were so detailed, precise and professional. Anyone would have thought she was a professional artist, but she wasn't.

Oh my gosh! I deviated big time, back to what I was originally writing about, spirit visitors in the night.

I've noticed the intensity of visitors and unusual occurrences at night has become really intense. I keep waking to a dark, strong and incredibly tall presence.

The only way to describe it is as a large mass of dark thick fog that feels dense, heavy and perhaps like a sticky dark treacle substance.

Well, I sound completely normal, not! It's peculiar for I feel no fear or troubled by its presence. It feels non-threatening, but also not exactly angelic. I should ask for it to show itself to me in a physical form, but I have a feeling that in time, it will show itself to me, but the time is not quite right yet.

I also have a feeling that when the time is right, I'll be shown its true form which I'm in no rush to discover.

Mediums see spiritual presences in human form, but I wonder if this is simply because we couldn't handle perhaps a different form, true form? The jury is still out on that thought! But I'm also not stupid enough to believe that all spiritual presences look like Bob or Barbara next door.

As long as it's not threatening and feels okay, I'll ignore it for now. I must admit I got quite shocked one of the nights as it was pitch black and I woke up still half asleep going to the toilet and this large black mass was standing directly behind me.

I jumped, but reacted almost as though it was normal, turned around and said, excuse me! It just didn't seem right to walk through it, so I found myself walking around it and getting back into bed.

How times really have changed, in the past I would have screamed, turned the light on and refused to turn them off until the morning. Anyway, this story doesn't end there. As I lay in bed, I'm in a light dream state. I find myself in a bright white room which I recognise as I've been here several times before.

I'm surrounded by a team of medics. I always recognise one of them for he looks a little like a mad professor with unruly hair and completely unthreatening. I can't see the others, I'm allowed to see their hands, but not their faces.

I should be freaking out, but also have a deep inner knowing this is part of my process and I choose to allow the process to continue.

Maybe this is an inner desperation of wanting to feel better in the real world. I'm sure that is what a trained psychologist would come up with. Although I don't know many people qualified to work out what goes on in a medium's world and certainly wouldn't value their opinion unless of course they were also an accomplished medium.

It's times like this I wish I had my old friend, Eddie, to talk to. He would tell me under no circumstances first to pull myself together and then the truth would come out whether I wanted to hear it or not. No flowering it up straight into the truth.

I'm smiling and laughing as I imagine Eddie's response.

Back to the medical room, as I'm lying there I can see the doctor holding my right arm. The doctor seems to be massaging the veins on my arm, the veins become more prominent as he does this procedure of tapping my arm in a strange way.

My veins look inhumanly large and elevated to the surface of my skin. Literally, they are bulging out, quite disgusting really.

The next minute, I'm being injected with a blue substance which initially makes my veins even more prominent and bluer.

My own blood is being released out of my arm as I can see the blood dripping from my hand. I'm watching all of this going on and not in the slightest bit concerned.

I'm tired and want the procedure to be finished for I know it's all part of a bigger plan.

I must have drifted off into a deeper sleep as I can't recall anything else. I wake up feeling a little bit uneasy with what I have seen and need to document it, why? Maybe, to write about it in this crazy book!

I spend the day analysing what has happened. Is any of this true? Surely, this has got to be just a dream and my imagination. I decided to compartmentalise the situation and not to give it any more thought.

What does it matter anyway? Who in their right mind

would believe all of this nonsense? I'm happy with my decision and will keep this one to myself. The problem is I can't deny the occurrence to myself because I've noticed several round dot bruises down this time the lower part of my right arm in rather precise formation.

There is no explanation for these bruises! I confide in my friend Clarissa, as I need the thoughts of a person who is gifted spiritually, grounded and not easily impressed with extra paranormal stuff unless she witnesses it for herself. Basically what I love about Clarissa is she is a no bullshit person and if she thinks you are talking rubbish, she will tell you.

I need someone to tell me this is fiction, not fact. As I tell Clarissa I can feel and sense she is not comfortable with the conversation, but she continues to listen. "Jane, I really don't know what is going on, but I also know you speak the truth. I wonder what it is they are doing with you, finely turning you but what for?"

I assure Clarissa this is true and that I can't make up physical precise round bruises by myself and even send her a photo. Clarissa confirms that she believes me for if it was untrue her guides would confirm I was a fruit loop.

We laugh about the situation and I say how mediumship is so easy and uncomplicated when you communicate with loved ones from the other side.

I've never had any interest in extra dimensional beings

for what is the point.

I know some people are fascinated and love paranormal activity but as much as it opens my mind, I can really say from my heart, it's not my cup of tea! I understand the importance of mediumship if in the right hands as it really does bring people comfort and healing.

The jury is out on the rest of this stuff which I can't prove exists or has any purpose yet. I decide to send up thoughts asking that all of this has a positive, loving and healing purpose for others. Otherwise, don't bother me!

So why ask Clarissa first and not Becky? Because Clarissa is a dedicated medium and only works to serve the spirit world in an honourable way. Clarissa will be guided by her spiritual team and immediately has the ability to spot the truth.

She might feel uncomfortable listening to my often unexplainable incidents, but she also has the desire to help.

More importantly, I need a friend who, like me, doesn't find this normal and can relate to why at times I find it unsettling. Also, I need to be believed!

I contacted Becky a few days later, she found it all very interesting and exciting. Just before she explains to me what has gone on she asks me to ask my guides first.

I suppose I haven't because I'm not sure I really want to know.

My guides assure me everything is fine and point out the precision of the markings and how nothing can harm me. This procedure is to ensure my energy can't be affected by others and I will never again in the future experience severe ill-health.

I am not to over analyse the situation and just trust. The procedure has been completed; they just need to finish off the final touches. All sounds very positive so why do I still feel dreadful? Mustn't complain as if there is one thing I know about my team, they only speak the truth and as much as I want to rush the procedure I know it is all on a timeline.

I ring Becky to tell her what has been discussed, she confirms she thought it wasn't appropriate for me to know too much knowledge for it could hinder my progression. We have a laugh about the situation and agree one day to discuss this process when I'm further down the line.

Becky is also a gifted medium who listens to the advice of her team. I see Becky in the future if she chooses to make the right decisions, talking in front of an audience sharing her knowledge and wisdom which will bring comfort and reassurance to those who have witnessed the same and need more understanding.

She will be successful within her own right in the future

and fulfil her life-long dream of working for the spirit world full-time.

TIME TO RETURN TO WORK

As I explained earlier in the book, Tony took some time off to help support my dreams. The reality of what I have seen in the future hasn't happened yet so as we all know, dreams and aspirations aren't always financially productive.

It has been a wonderful time reconnecting as a family also I've been reminded how lucky I am to have such a supportive friend and husband. I'm also grateful that he is level-headed, sees the world and life slightly differently from me.

I often wonder what it would be like to have a partner who was equally into spiritual stuff. I can honestly say I wouldn't find it attractive for I really need someone different to me in my life to keep things real.

Within a few weeks, Tony is back in the rat race of the material world. I won't lie, it's rather comforting knowing there is money coming back into the home.

I just hope he can manage to keep the work-life balance more healthy this time. It's a comforting position to be in for I don't see Tony working so hard in the future, well not for someone else. This just feels like a chapter or stepping stone until hopefully my work takes off.

My health is improving and I'm starting to get more energy and have the urge to push the boundaries by participating in challenging myself to stand up in front of people to demonstrate mediumship. Baby steps, but I must start getting my confidence back and most of all, start believing in myself.

I have this deep knowing that as much as I fear standing in front of people whether that be mediumship demonstrations or public speaking I have to get used to it, for much to my horror if the future I have seen comes to reality I've got to learn pretty quickly how to stop going bright red and speaking too quickly.

My fear of speaking in public stems from my childhood memories of being forced to read aloud in the classroom where there was no compassion for failure, just good old fashioned ridicule. What is it they say, no pain, no gain!

As an adult, I now disagree and believe nurture and encouragement outweigh those old teaching methods. I find it really disappointing that teachers are still using the random finger pointing at students in class which is great for the confident child, but destroys the more sensitive and shy child.

I have spoken to particular teachers about this on several occasions regarding one of my own children being unable to focus in class due to the fear of randomly being fired questions at.

The teachers have been very understanding and stopped this approach to my child resulting in my child feeling safe, happy, confident and able to learn in the classroom, but I do worry for those children who feel the same and feel too embarrassed to discuss this with their parents.

I've also been told by the teachers that this method is standard and still encouraged and taught to newly qualified teachers. We have got to start decreasing the mental obstacles at school and start thinking outside the box.

The last thing an adolescent, body-conscious child needs is to be highlighted in class. The reply I have been given by the teacher is this ensures the children are listening. Well, just a suggestion, be a little more fun, positive and engaging and then you will capture even the most bored child. This method punishes the sensitive child.

Sensitive children need to feel safe and perhaps given more time to develop their confidence. As I have said, the teachers I have highlighted this to were very understanding and kind which to be honest I wasn't expecting.

Why have I waffled on with this? In the hope it will resonate with perhaps a teacher or even better a parent who can start the conversation with their own child. If we don't ask one another how we really feel and dig a little deeper, we can't learn.

PREDICTION

I wasn't going to share this, but have been told I must.
Another session of unsettling healing if that's what you
want to call it occurs. As I lie relaxing in a meditative
state, the usual movements and adjustments start to
take place, no longer bothered, I just succumb to the
process.

Suddenly, I experience the most horrendous sharp pain
in my left eye that literally takes my breath away. I feel
uneasy and to be perfectly honest, scared. This is the
first time in ages I question my physical safety.

I calm myself down and tell myself I am completely safe
for they have invested too much time in my
development and purpose whatever that is to be?

As I lie there, I feel incredibly nauseous due to a mixture
of fear and to be frank, horror. My left eyeball feels like
it is being moved and needs to come out. I feel the
tissues supporting the eye being manipulated and
visualise it being pushed forwards, yes, removed but
still connected by veins, ligaments and connective
tissue.

I become tired and think, just bloody get on with it and
then have a sudden change of heart and panic and
refuse to give permission. The pain instantly vanishes,
calmness is restored in the room and once again, I'm
strangely calm and accepting of the situation which

unsettles me more than having my eyeball played with.

As I write this information, I think of my poor parents reaction if ever I should release this book. They are accepting of my mediumship, but this is a little bit too much even for them. My poor Mum, having to pretend to be proud of her daughter's new book, especially as her side of the family are pretty normal.

I'll cross that bridge when it occurs. I know she will hide the book from my father as I have a funny feeling he hasn't been allowed to read the first book. My poor mother!

As I have mentioned before, I have been shown my future which is going to be let's say unconventional and challenging. I will be invited onto a well-known TV show and interviewed which brings me nothing but indescribable shudders of horror.

I am such a private person hardly anyone knows anything about me other than I am a respectable mum of three.

Why would anyone choose to even admit to all of these crazy events? I have spoken to my spiritual team about this and agreed to do it, but only if I am one hundred percent healthy and my energy levels are completely back to normal so I can deal with the ordeal and potentially the ridicule.

So, I suppose pulling my eyeball out and replacing it to

complete the healing process is a must, yikes! I often wonder what it would be like not to have any of this thought-provoking activity. I can honestly say which I appreciate sounds a little concerning, I wouldn't change a thing.

I'm convinced that what I write will help others, surely that is a good thing?

Nobody wants to feel they are alone in the world. Well, let me tell you the reader, nobody is alone and that is a promise!

We are surrounded by so many on the other side whether you choose to believe or not, including loved ones. I hope that brings comfort to someone who genuinely feels lonely.

I'm trying to work out when I need to release this next book. My first plan was never, second, when I could prove some of what I had written was real, thirdly, probably when it is complete to prove the final outcome.

The reality is as always, my spirit team will tell me and I just have to trust. What is it I want out of these books being released? I'm not convinced I can fully answer that at the moment for I'm not convinced I truthfully know.

I'm pretty mortified that at some point I will have to take ownership of these last two 'reluctant medium' books, but it feels like a tradeoff to get people more interested in reading the other books I have channelled from spirit.

The channelled books I have written are directly from spirit, which are far superior than anything I could or would claim to be able to write. The writings are healing, thought-provoking, simple and for some have reduced them to tears and deeply resonated with them.

I'm not deluded, I can see perhaps why I have to write about my journey as it will appeal to more people.

I hope it will help others and by the emails I have received from the first book, it would imply this. It feels like a weird trade off, fascinating the public with your private journey (sell your soul!) to get people to read the less exciting, channelled writings that can genuinely help them.

There are so many people who crave recognition, fame, material gain and yet I crave none of the above. I think it would be funny to be associated as a writer, as I'm not a writer or from an academic background. This would really amuse my often sick military sense of humour which I have learnt to disguise, only allowing free in the right company.

I laugh at the prospect of one of my old school teachers who often looked at me with pity in their eyes, feeling they actually knew me as a real living person of little academia.

How could this be, a child who struggled to read, write a bloody book, grammatically horrendously incorrect and people enjoy it?

An outrage! I WOULD LOVE THAT! A couple of years ago, a well-known book made millions and I remember the outraged comments about this person's lack of written skills. So what, good on that person, how about well done you!

The fact of the matter is this person wrote in a way people could relate to, not in fancy words or correct grammatically, but in her words. Wouldn't it be nice if as humans we could learn to wish another well and genuinely mean it? I love seeing people succeed and being happy. I struggle with why so many of us can't be happy for one another.

I take my hat off to those who are celebrities for they have lost the choice of total privacy of their lives. I understand fame to help others, but not just for material gain, opulence and simply needing to be embraced by strangers.

Strangers, don't actually know you so, probably don't really give a shit about you. A bit harsh, but it's the truth.

When I hear the abuse some celebrities are subjected to on social media, especially when it is about their appearance, it really makes me sad. I literally have only been subjected to a few arseholes on social media and decided not to bother with it, for I can't stress enough we are not here very long, so why subject yourself to abuse?

We are all made up of energy and have a choice to sever the ties. Unless you really need followers to put food on the table and a roof over your head, I simply don't understand the desire. I can see how an innocent and naive younger person might believe this is what you should do as that is what they are led to believe in society, but not for a middle-aged woman, no thank you!

Thank goodness there isn't a picture of me out there. Would you want to be associated with this book? NO! I've decided I'm not going to waste anymore of my time worrying about the future, ifs, buts and maybes for these are only feelings and thoughts and not real, yet!

LUCID DREAMING BECOMING UNCOMFORTABLY REAL.

I'm in a house, I don't recognise it, but I've been here before. There is a young boy aged nine with brown hair lying exhausted in a bed. The whole room feels heavy, I can see he has been lying in the bed for quite some time as the bed covers are twisted and it smells of stale body odour.

The child is so tired he can barely move. There is no medical explanation, just an overpowering sense of fatigue. The child has lost the will to fight, fatigued and in the depths of darkness, he just wants to sleep.

I speak to the mother who I immediately recognise, she is worried sick because the school has been relentlessly contacting them for without a medical letter her son must attend school.

My friend is also tired, but I can feel a heightened anxiety and mixture of fear gathering momentum around her.

There is an overwhelming feeling of darkness and sadness burrowed deeply hidden within her for I can feel all her emotions. She explains to me she just can't do this anymore; she can't get him out of bed.

There is a knock at the door, a female teacher bursts through the door. She takes over the whole room bringing in a class full of children. "Well, if you can't get your child to school, then I will bring the class to your home."

She says in a dictatorial and very aggressive manner. I'm stood watching the process before my very eyes, utterly shocked by the arrogance and rudeness of this woman.

I identify there is more going on with my friend's feelings for now she can't escape and feels trapped and vulnerable within her own home. Watching the invasion of my friend's home starts to make me feel angry and overprotective.

Who is this woman to violate another's sacred space, another's home? The boy just lies there still unable to move seemingly lifeless. The pompous teacher has no compassion and an inability to see the needs of the family in this situation for she has a job to do and by hook or crook, she will do it.

Her authority demands respect as she takes over the whole room. I feel annoyed because my friend is soft, gentle, so tired and fragile by the demands of life!

I can't stand by and watch the intimidation of this woman towards my friend anymore, "GET OUT! You have no respect and no right to enter another person's home," I said.

The teacher turns, looks me straight in the eyes and just before she is about to make a comment, I feel overwhelmed with authority and power and say clearly directly into her face, "GET OUT, NOW!"

The woman is shocked and furious because I should respect her position of importance and authority. I feel liberated and enjoy my newfound strength. More importantly, I will not stand by to see another intimidated, especially not in her own home.

The whole situation starts to calm down, the teacher leaves with her very well-behaved, frightened and controlled class of children.

As the room settles down, I look over to my right to see a male teacher sitting on a stool by a kitchen island watching the whole process. I don't know him in the material world, but I know him! I know I have served with him in a previous military life and we are close comrades.

He has broad athletic shoulders, short dark brown hair and is wearing a casual T-shirt. He is very handsome and as I look into his eyes I feel such a familiarity it fills me with love and contentment. He feels calm, gentle and wise. I don't allow many people to truly know me, but he knows and understands me better than myself.

We sit on the floor side by side where I notice he has lost his legs, this doesn't surprise me for I already somehow know this. We talk so freely, so comfortable in each other's space, he is funny, relatable, knowledgeable and intriguing.

I have an overwhelming spiritual connection and an attraction to him, but not in a human, physical form. I feel so safe, protected, at home and blissfully happy.

He senses my ease and moves a little closer. I can feel his shoulder touch mine, it's not uncomfortable or embarrassing. I want his shoulder to touch mine, I crave his touch and presence. His head touches mine which again is okay. I feel so safe and comforted.

The spiritual connection can't be articulated for there are no words to describe other than none of this is sexual or physical. Anyone that knows me would know if it didn't feel pure, I would have run a mile down the road by now.

His face and head move closer to mine where I can physically feel the warmth of his face and shoulder gently hugging mine in a loving, gentle movement. I don't want it to stop because his touch is pure, healing and loving. I never want this moment to stop.

As I sit there the whole of my head and left side of my shoulder girdle has this tingling, warmth that is unusual to anything I have ever felt or experienced before. No! I can feel myself starting to wake up. I'm in a daze, but I can still feel the warmth and tingling sensation. I hear loudly the words, "Let go, just go with it!"

I feel no desire to move and know I am being directed to keep still. I am fully awake lying in bed with my eyes closed enjoying the tingling and warmth which is still being activated in my upper shoulder, neck and head. I decided not to overthink and just enjoy the process.

As I lie there, I can feel the deep muscular tissues being released physically in the left side of my chest and a heavy shadow substance being gently moved. I see a web-like see-through veil detaching from my chest and being removed. As it is removed it fades and vanishes into the atmosphere. I continue to lie very still until the process, warmth and tingling stops which remains for a further minute.

I lie there speechless, I've seen lots of unconventional happenings, but never for this length of time, fully awake and physical in the material world. My mind starts to wonder, "Why are they letting me witness this?" Then I lie there trying to work out the process I have just witnessed so I can at least make sense of it to myself.

I basically can't, so I decide to put this experience in another box and explain it as another layer has simply been removed from me so I can progress forwards further in this lifetime. I like to think perhaps there is lots of healing going on in the world to each and every one of us, only a few of us get to physically witness it.

As I analyse the situation, I feel very emotional, tired and thankful. I send a thought out into the universe thanking whatever it is, God, loving divine for all the time and healing that has been invested in me.

There has to be more to all of this, I can't prove it yet but I have a deep knowing there is something and I will find out what it is in this lifetime, surely?

Something after that experience has settled and calmed me down. I have no more fight or desire to push against who I am. I feel content that there is a process bigger and more powerful than me that will ensure I get over the finish line.

I can see a finish line, maybe it's time to accept perhaps I'm not completely in control of my destiny. Some say we agree to a plan or contract before we are born. I don't know, but I suspect this journey would be more enjoyable if I learn to trust and go with it! I'll try and see how long I last!

I must admit I'm a little concerned to see my friend appear in my dream, but more alarmed how much mentally she is struggling. I have this sinking sensation in the pit of my stomach that something awful has happened and I'm ashamed to admit I feel almost reluctant to ring her for I also know I can't help her. I'll ring her in a few days and check she is okay.

SWAN LAKE

I have a grand total of two days of feeling calmer and more in control of life! I've even had two nights of not being disturbed by wacky dreams or any visitors in the night and I'm loving it! I feel a little smug with myself.

It is so rare, but occasionally I pass out and sleep so deeply there is nothing, black, silent and a beautiful nothingness. I wake up and feel so uplifted and pleased with myself that I have had complete rest and silence.

I'm not deluded. I'm sure I have been off astral travelling or doing something crazy, but I just bathe in the fact I've had silence, no running around in another world or any dreams. Some people are frightened of being on their own in silence, I love it!

It's quite amusing if you watch people's behaviour, they seem to congratulate themselves for being busy all the time.

I'm a real people watcher, when my children were very young, under 5, so many parents would rush around making sure their children were entertained all the time.

There were the weekly music fun time sessions, gym tot times, outings to the farm, the list went on. How do I know this, because I was one of those parents.

The times I gave the children a chill out day at home they were equally as happy not to be rushing around, stimulated by relentless noise and interaction.

In fact, I discovered the majority of the classes were actually for the parents socially more than the child. The point I'm trying to make is that it is okay to spend time in the quiet, in fact, it's healthy and necessary for everyone's mental well-being.

Yet we are all guilty of getting on the wheel of the rat race believing what we are sold by other's views or society, this is how we should behave. I spoke to a friend of mine who has four children and she was literally busy all the time, it really looked exhausting from the outside looking in.

One day, we were chatting and I asked her why she felt she had to do so much with her kids and never had time at home. The answer was refreshingly honest, she said because it was so much harder to stay indoors, not for the children, but for her.

Her children were always doing something and had almost lost the ability to slow down and just be content at home which had resulted in my poor friend never getting a break.

Home should be a place to relax and escape this often busy and over sensory world, but if we don't allow ourselves a safe place to just be, by this I mean a quiet place to unwind and hear our own thoughts, feelings and emotions, then as a species we are literally stuffed!

The next time you go out for a coffee, sit and watch people rushing around, look at their expressions. Listen to all the sounds around you, look at all the artificial lights and bright signs trying to get your attention. I would question if our environments are conducive to our mental well-being?

I think it is sad so many of us accept this as normal. Especially those rushing around continually, not allowing themselves the pleasure and simplicity of nature, the wind upon your skin, the time to breathe in deeply.

I also have a suspicion that some people, whether they would admit it or not, are scared to sit in the quiet and address their true feelings or past events.

Nature is free, costs nothing and more effective than any man-made manufactured drug, but takes the individual to make time to step outside and feel the elements of nature. I'm not suggesting for one moment certain individuals don't need medication, for some it is literally a game-changer and for some a life-saver.

It just frustrates me that we live in a world where everything appears reactive, especially to mental health rather than preventative. Prevention is always better than cure!

There seems to be limited help until the person

becomes so-called broken and then it is decided, wait for it, whether that poor person suffering is considered broken enough to warrant help.

Prevention also takes time, care and nurture which some might argue our medical professionals haven't got time for. Think of all the happy content people and the millions of pounds our country could save if we changed the current system to a preventative care system. (Just another opinion!)

I have another hope for the future. I hope society will go full circle and learn to accept we have our own minds, opinions and a deeper understanding of what is right and healing for us as a species.

I believe the time is coming when we will stop becoming absorbed by what we are fed to be true and work out this journey for ourselves which in turn will help our children. Oh my gosh, preachy! I can't stand preachy people, yikes I just became one. (Just my view, anyway, back to the book.)

Back to Swan Lake, I'm lying on the floor (This is a dream) dying next to a man who I don't know in the material world, but I know him in another dimension or the dream world. I'm safe and have no fear, but I don't want this man with me at the end of my life. I want my Tony!

I'm searching frantically for my Tony, I'm not leaving this world without my Tony by my side. Tony appears, I feel blissfully happy, calm, content and happy to pass over for I know we will be reunited. I hear with such clarity music being played, it's comforting and also I immediately recognise it as 'Swan Lake.' I have a knowing and greater depth of understanding my old self is being released.

I physically wake up, I see a face of a lady from the spirit world with dark hair who I have never met, trying to get my attention. I immediately think of my friend in the previous dream and know her mother has died. I have to contact my friend, but what do I say? I'm scared to know the truth, but I must. What sort of friend am I if I can't be there?

Without going into detail as you might have gathered by the way I write, I don't reveal personal details of others out of respect. But I can tell you my friend's mother had died, I couldn't make anything better, the atmosphere was of great sadness, tiredness and despair. Her mother was worried and had, through pure love and determination made me, make that call.

I was also forbidden to make any form of connection to the spiritual world until my friend had processed her loss and allowed the healing to begin. Another lesson: don't run away from what is right, even if at times you might feel scared, another's needs are often far more important than yours.

We arranged a coffee catch up and that's when it was

officially confirmed her mother had recently passed over, it was so sad. Her world had fallen apart and the pain she was feeling was unbearable. I desperately wanted to make everything better, even if I could just take the edge of her pain and connect to her mother to assure her, her mother was safe, happy and well.

I was told firmly by my guides, under no circumstances was I allowed to. I was permitted to listen, nothing more, nothing less, just listen. I felt helpless, but just hoped by simply listening it would help in any way, for I am naturally a fixer and wanted to bring healing and comfort.

I was forbidden, it wasn't rocket science to work out because my friend was in a very dark, sad and suffocating place. When the time is right, I will be guided, but I knew not to interfere until my friend was in a better place and had processed the grieving and started to heal.

A medium can do more damage than good if they don't respect the individual's healing process. My good friend Eddie would always repeat the words, "You can't heal everyone and nor should you try."

A highly thought of medium who will not be named told us a harrowing story in our closed development circle (a closed development circle consists of a group of generally more advanced mediums who commit to meeting weekly to perfect the connection to the spirit world seeking evidential facts).

A lady came to visit her for a reading and had ensured her the medium, enough time had passed to grieve the loss of her husband. This lady seemed well educated, of sound mind and just wanted to know her husband was safe in the spirit world.

The medium assessed the situation and felt the lady was telling the truth and gave her no reason to believe otherwise. The lady was blown away by the accuracy of the reading, she felt reassured there was an afterlife and no longer feared for her husband's happiness on the other side. My friend felt honoured she had been able to bring comfort to this lady.

Within a matter of days, there was a knock at the door of the medium's house. The police were investigating the death of the lady who had previously visited the medium.

The evidence this lady had received was so precise she no longer questioned there was an afterlife and unfortunately, she wanted to be with her husband and took her own life.

She left a child behind who later contacted the medium who screamed into the medium's face that she was a murderer!

The medium was investigated by the police and there was no evidence any of this was the medium's fault.

To this day, the medium has to live with those words shouted in her face. As much as mediums bring healing, closure and contentment, if you have any feeling the time is not right or not given permission by your spiritual team, you must obey.

Mediumship is not for entertainment for with it comes a huge responsibility. Very rarely does someone choose to visit a medium for fun, if they do they should be sent away. Mediumship is not for entertainment!

CAN IT GET ANY WORSE?

I wasn't going to mention any more strange healing sessions, but this one was a little too extreme not to mention. Let's face it, I can't possibly sound any more unhinged than what I have already written. What is it they say, in for a penny, in for a pound?

Here goes, feeling happy with life, keep getting told by my spiritual guides I'm nearly at the finish line. When I hear this, I often reply with, "That's nice" for I've heard it all before and believe it or not I'm actually quite a logical person and like proof.

I don't doubt my future health, but I have also resorted to accepting it's on a timeline and I'm not about to get excited about future finish lines until I'm over the line.

Out of the blue, my left ear becomes worse, to the point I can't sleep through the pain due to the throbbing. It's funny when your health deteriorates you suddenly learn the lesson of how much more thankful you should have been for the level of health you had before and to appreciate everything, for you don't know if there will be periods of your health getting worse.

The pain starts to radiate over to the right, my hearing is reduced and I can hear high frequency pitches like I'm a finely tuned radio being played with and adjusted. I decided to ring the doctor for surely this must be an ear infection.

The doctor asks me if I have been swimming recently or felt run down because it is unusual for an ear infection to materialise at my age with no reason. I'm given ear drop antibiotics that make my ear worse and now find myself in excruciating pain.

I ring the doctor again and I'm given oral antibiotics which give me hope of settling the pain. I lose the feeling in the left side of my face whilst I have this awful knowing the frequency inside my head is being altered. What should I do?

I can't ring the doctor again and I'm certainly not going to try and explain frequencies are being adjusted in my head. I just have to accept the process and pray it will finish soon. I find myself lying in bed for prolonged periods of time because I really don't know what to do with myself.

Finally, I fall asleep, only to be woken up to the left side of my tongue being physically pinched and startling me. The fun begins, my head is violently thrown around almost like trying to shift fluid within my skull. I know from experience this is not a time to fight the process for I could do more damage than good.

My head is put into an end range position putting an increased strain on the vertebrae in my neck. I feel scared as out of nowhere, I recall something I learnt on my remedial instructor's course whilst serving in the military.

The saying went C5 stay alive which basically means any severe damage to the cervical above C5 (upper bones of the spine around the neck area) could result in death or being paralysed!

I quickly console myself that there is no benefit in anything other than a positive outcome in this situation for too much time has been invested in me. More importantly, my guides have protected me throughout my life and I've seen the bigger picture.

I suddenly feel a warmth of reassurance and an increased blood flow around my head and upper body. I'm so tired physically and mentally of these occurrences, but what is the alternative? I know everything will be fine and I'm shown a clear card from the tarot card deck of a straight path ahead, but feel emotional and plead for this to end.

The pain within my right ear drum feels under so much pressure, it feels like a sharp object is being plunged into the ear canal. I'm almost wishing the ear would burst to stop the pain. "Please, just make the pain stop!" I'm begging within my mind.

My eyes start to flicker which increases to a strong force pushing my eyeballs back into the sockets, the eyes feel fatigued as though I can't physically cope with the sensation and discomfort, yet I have no control over the process.

My eyes are restricted so far back it goes black, as the

intensity is reduced there are a multitude of different colours that I have never seen before or can identify.

Finally, the intensity of pain settles. I lie there lifeless, pale, clammy and in a fever-like state.

"What the hell has just happened?" I hear the words it's almost time to move home and move forwards.

I physically want to cry because the pain was so intense, but I'm so tired, I simply can't.

"Why are you doing this to me?" I begged them to finish the process and asked them, "Why me, this is cruel, I don't want to do this anymore." I hear their reply in my mind, "Because Jane, you are strong, courageous, committed and won't be defeated. It must be you!" I hear my mind respond that I will not be beaten and that I cannot be destroyed!

Strange, because that's not how I am physically feeling. This is all very nice, but my head is in a right old mess, the left side of my body feels pretty good which is a first.

I feel mentally alert and the foggy sensation in my head has been removed. The right side of my body, which used to be my good side, feels battered, sore, bruised and I can't hear a thing. Oh, the joys of this flipping journey!

Whilst re-reading this book, I remembered Eddie telling

me he had throughout his life gone to the doctors several times convinced he had ear infections and heard frequent high pitched noises in his ears.

The doctors would find nothing wrong with him and I remember Eddie making facial expressions re-enacting the doctor as he looked at Eddie with sympathy and concern as though he was obviously lacking something emotional in his life.

Eddie eventually cottoned on; it was just the spirit world adjusting the frequency allowing him clearer communication between the two worlds. The advice from Eddie was, "You have to get used to it and learn to live with it."   I had genuinely forgotten about that conversation with Eddie, but I imagine he is having a little laugh at this.

AN OPPORTUNITY TO CONFORM
AND BE NORMAL!

It's December 2021 and I have this lovely contentment and inner feeling of calmness and dare I say it, self-acceptance. I've been having recurring dreams about finding a job and keep finding myself back in a military environment. It's such a relief when I wake up to realise I have escaped that regimented environment.

I understand my dreams, feelings and thoughts. I can easily identify it is due to my impatience to be well enough to find a place in this world, a little guilt perhaps of being a stay-at-home mum. I hate the reaction from other women when they find out you are a stay-at-home mum, almost a look of bemusement.

What is wrong with her, her children are at school, lazy cow! I would love to say actually, I'm a medium, I spent a lot of my time channelling from the spirit world and please don't look at me with pity as I can easily pick up in your energy as much as you are telling me your life is perfect and you are an amazing hardworking mother, wife, lover and on social media everything is perfect, you are feeling run ragged, unappreciated and shattered.

I always smile and agree with how amazing they are because if it gives them self-importance and happiness, then why not. Women can be each other's worst nightmare. When I say I am a stay-at-home mum, they immediately justify how their work fulfils them and couldn't possibly do nothing!

Nothing that's a strange thing to say to a stay-at-home mum, I can't recall doing nothing. I often wonder if it's a protective mechanism as maybe they secretly would like more time with their family or is society again dictating what we are led to believe will fulfil us. How about all you women that work and juggle so much, WELL DONE, YOU! And to all those full-time mums who work for no financial gain, WELL DONE, YOU TOO!

Whatever an individual woman decides to do there are always sacrifices so how about we just support one another and don't judge. What is right for one person isn't always right for another. Back to my recurring dreams, I know these are due to frustration of not moving forwards with my health quick enough and secretly I suppose wanting to conform to this material world.

I also know I'm not supposed to have a normal job and would be utterly bored and frustrated after a couple of months, but that doesn't seem to stop the idea I have created and desire to fit in with society. I go for my three monthly back check-up, whilst lying there the lovely lady who is treating me randomly says, "Jane, would you like a job? I need a receptionist, you are really good with people, you would be perfect."

Well, I didn't see that one coming. I replied I hadn't given it any thought and would have a think about it. I discussed it with my mother who thought it would be a wonderful idea and felt relieved that finally her daughter would put all this spiritual nonsense to bed and live in the real world. I discussed it with Tony, who looked amused, but would support me with whatever I decided.

I felt honoured that someone had offered me a job, but also had an overwhelming feeling of nothing, no excitement and secretly knew it wasn't for me. I spoke to my children about it, one asked how much I would earn. Another reminded me that I was supposed to do what I was good at and that was working with spirit and the last one really wasn't interested but said, you are already working as a writer and to do what makes you happy.

Surely if I took the job, I would be a good example to my kids? The next week I spent in turmoil, spending time writing pros and cons lists. The problem was I felt an inner sadness of knowing all this job would do would distract me from what I should be doing, writing. My guides said take the job if you want, but all we want from you is to write.

I needed to speak to my friend Clarissa, she would be honest and would only want what's best for me. I told Clarissa my dilemma and she immediately burst out laughing. "You! as a bloody receptionist! That's the last thing in the world I expected you to come out with. Is that going to get you to your dream?

Firstly, your health hasn't fully returned, you will be in a working environment where you will be picking up everyone's energy making them all feel better, but what about your health? You would be better off doing readings than doing this. I have a question, what would excite you more, perhaps doing readings on the telephone where you could still hide your identity or working as a receptionist?" said Clarissa.

Any form of spiritual work excites and fulfils me. I immediately got a flutter and excitement in my heart.

Clarissa went on to say, "Jane, you are in a position to be able to do what you want, a receptionist, really!" and then proceeded to giggle.

We did laugh as I told her how excited my mother was that finally her child was to return to the real world and how proud she would have been to tell her friends. That was a close one. I literally nearly became normal, yikes! It didn't feel good.

So, I politely declined the offer of the job which was a wonderful feeling for I had nearly done what society had expected of me, but I had taken control and made my own decision on my future. I felt empowered, my focus and path had become crystal clear. I would continue writing and then after Christmas, I would go and get myself a job doing spiritual readings.

I had a plan, I had clarity and an inner acceptance that it was okay to be me. I didn't need to conform to what I thought was expected of me, it was finally alright to be me! I also knew I needed to continue writing for I was regularly and firmly reminded by my spirit guides not to complicate things.

The thought of another year of just writing wasn't enough, I had made my choice, I would shake things up and start doing readings. The funny thing was I had always promised myself I would never work for a psychic company as I had if I'm being honest looked down upon it, yet it was almost as though I needed to experience it.

Where would I start, I would have to work for a legit company and more importantly one that didn't exploit people's vulnerabilities. Clarissa was all over it, she already knew of two good companies and assured me they were the best, only employed the best and I would be tested, scrutinised and have to pass several obstacles.

Clarissa warned me one of the companies was exceptionally hard to get into and apparently statistically only took one out of two hundred applicants and paid the best. I wasn't sure this was true, but Clarissa always researched her facts meticulously.

The alternative was I could pick one of the less known companies and not have the pressure, but if I was going to work for a company, they had to not only be the best, have a high code of moral values and more important, the real deal. I would put this thought to bed and review it after Christmas.

LIFE CONTINUES

I feel happier writing and starting to feel the joy in it again as I know after Christmas, I will introduce more variety. My health is slowly improving and I decide it is time to take the next step and start doing spiritual workshops to see how my health responds.

I decided the group I had been attending in lockdown on Zoom is perfect for they are experienced mediums but more importantly incredibly kind.

A group of people who make you feel welcome, it is safe to show weakness, vulnerability and to be your unapologetic self.

The first workshop I decide to go on is about tarot cards. I feel apprehensive because it's a six-hour course and I usually have to lie down during the day in the middle of the course. As soon as we get the opportunity to work, I feel alive, my guides come straight in and the words flow from my mouth.

The cards are a great tool, it's good to know what the cards mean but it is just a guide. I have read several books on the story and history of the tarot cards which is fascinating, but there is actually no proof of any of it being true and once again,the history doesn't help with reading the cards that comes from the ability of the reader.

It's simply another tool to enhance what you already have and that is basically the connection between you and your guides. Anyone can read the cards, but what you must remember is, what one card means doesn't mean the same for everyone.

If you read the same card for ten different people, it should mean the same, but it doesn't. Every individual is unique so how can one card be the same for everyone? The answer is, it might have the same initial meaning, but then that meaning becomes individual for each person.

When I read, my spirit team draws my eyes to a part of the card and then the words just flow, so basically my team uses me as a channel. The accuracy is so much more precise than just learning the meaning of set cards although this is still very important for if you are going to use the tarot, you should use it properly and in time with experience it really can become a beautiful form of art.

The images of a little old lady at the funfair are hopefully coming to an end, for the tarot is being used more as a guidance and a form of almost life coaching. I don't like to just play at things, I have a thirst to understand and learn from the best so that is what I have done.

I've searched out the best tarot card reader, psychic/medium in the business, enrolled in an in depth course to learn advanced methods, professional codes of conduct, using tarot as a means of helping people in the current times.

When tarot is used in a professional way it can have a huge, positive impact on another's life. So actually I correct myself, if you are going to read using the tarot cards, it is your responsibility to learn as much as you can, but more importantly no one can ever be hundred percent correct so don't answer questions that can shatter people's lives.

If someone says, "Will I divorce my husband? you would say, "Would you like to look at your relationship?" I have no right to say, sorry love, it's over. The client already knows all the answers; they just need someone literally to guide them.

I find the tarot a pleasure to work with for it plays to my strengths as a medium, but still I've searched out the best mentor because it's so important to me to do things properly. I didn't need to, but I'm glad I did for you never stop learning in this life.

I also love learning from experienced spiritually-gifted people. I find gifted people fascinating—how their minds work and it enables my own thoughts to be challenged. I always make the decision on what knowledge I retain and if in doubt with what I hear and if it often doesn't resonate, I simply disregard it.

The other thing whilst I'm rambling away is just because

a person works in a certain way doesn't mean it will work for you and you mustn't become a clone. Always be your authentic, true self!

So, as I have said, if you say you are reading the tarot, you must learn the meaning of the cards first, but not become a robot for the clever bit is your intuition. I enjoy the cards because it's not as intense as solely working as a medium and you can move in and out of energies.

What do I mean by this? Basically, using your knowledge, feeling and working in the spiritual energy and using your intuition to read the cards. Not to forget the energy of the person in front of you.

Finally, if you have the ability, the clever bit is to channel exactly what the person needs to hear to move forwards in a positive and uplifting way. Working in this way is still tiring, for you are still being used as a channel but usually with your spirit team which I find much lighter to work with.

The client should always leave feeling satisfied with the reading, but more importantly, optimistic. I personally find working as a medium and allowing other people's deceased loved ones to use me as a channel at the moment exhausting.

Whilst I'm working, I am full of heightened energy and feel fantastic but then a few hours later, I'm floored with exhaustion.

I have been assured by my spiritual team that in the future this will improve and I will no longer experience such physical and mental fatigue. I hear lots of mediums in uproar and saying you are not protecting yourself properly.

Yes, you could be right, but also I have a knowing on the spiritual side that they are still finetuning me and that takes time, hence I'm sticking to writing until the process is completed. God help you all, when I'm finally fully fit to work,

I'm probably going to be an over excited pain in the arse. I can't bloody wait, but for the time being, I must listen. I'm excited by the prospect of not hiding who I truly am anymore and I am not ever going to apologise for being a little different.

I really wish I hadn't wasted so much of my time worrying about others' opinions, that self-loathing feeling of embarrassment of who I am. I feel sad for the years wasted on fear and the thoughts of ridicule, especially in my child years of myself, but then I'm blessed for some in this lifetime don't or refuse to accept themselves for their true self. So hey, better late than never!

Sorry, I deviated again.

The most important thing when reading for others is to remember these are real people who often come to you because they might be struggling in life and I believe whatever you uncover you do not ever leave a person on a negative. I will continue reading until I discover a positive, I have never to this day not discovered a positive in a person's life.

Out of every hardship, lessons are learnt. It really is how you perceive the journey. As much as the tarot is a good tool, once again it all depends on whose hands it is in. I have attended courses before and often thought this could do more damage than good, especially with someone who just learns the meaning of the cards and hasn't got any psychic or spiritual ability.

Back to the tarot workshop, I'm loving the day, I waver between feeling energetic and on a high to periods when I'm not connecting spiritually to feeling exhausted, nauseous with a headache, but I'm determined I'm going to do the whole day.

When I'm working, I feel so happy because it's the only time I truly feel I'm doing what I'm supposed to do.

The reward, feelings and sensation of connecting with my spiritual team is how can I put it?

Humbling and an honour. I do several readings which I feel have gone well but always question whether I could have perhaps done better.

One of my faults is I'm a little self-critical and always strive for perfection. When you work spiritually, you are to remove all ego and self-doubt and just trust. I'm still working on this and perhaps will throughout this lifetime.

The instructor noticed my work, implied I was good and said I should be charging or there should be an exchange of some sort. Those words meant the world to me for being a hidden medium sometimes, you need to hear you are okay, even good at what you do.

I've noticed throughout the day there were so many talented mediums in the room, generally over the age of fifty five upwards so I was a youngster. One thing we all had in common was it didn't matter how much evidence we produced, the majority weren't overly confident people, a little naturally quieter and sensitive.

If you met me, you would laugh at this statement for I come across as confident and self-assured, but that is not the true me. That is thanks to my military training and being taught the art of appearing in control.

I love people watching and meeting new people because I genuinely find people's life stories fascinating. The workshop finally finishes, Tony has arrived to pick me up as I'm not quite well enough to drive long journeys.

I'm feeling on a high and telling Tony how proud I feel that I've completed a six-hour workshop and really feel I've achieved something today. On the drive back home, I feel awful as the colour drains from my cheeks and the inner swirl of unbalance begins to increase inside my body.

I feel so drained, the fatigue is hard to describe other than I just don't know what to do with myself as I feel overwhelmed with a sense, I need to be sick. It saddens me that the one thing that lifts my soul and fulfils me completely for some reason also drains the life out of me.

As soon as I get home, it's straight to bed to recharge. Tony looks at me with concern and love in his eyes, but also knows not to say a word. Tony is the only person who has seen and witnessed how ill I have been over the last six years.

He understands more than anyone how it has been drilled into us during our military careers not to show weakness and appear in control to the outside world. Behind closed doors and only at home, it is safe to crumble.

I have tried to explain how poorly I have been to a few people, but find it awkward, embarrassing and uncomfortable, especially as I look well, always turn up, put on makeup and a big smile. They listen, but they don't really hear what I am saying and I suppose why should they?

For unless they have had the same experience, they simply can't understand. Sometimes, I think maybe if I just stopped showering, lay in bed and finally gave up I would be taken seriously.

I can't do this because I fear and know the power of the depths of that black hole and how if I allowed myself to succumb, it could swallow me up and possibly I would lose the ability to return to normality. I have on many occasions taken pleasure in the thought of doing this, refusing to get out of bed and just allowing myself to stop completely, but thank goodness the love and needs of others must always come first.

It takes a couple of days to recover after that workshop, but do you know what, it was bloody worth it. I'm a great believer in balance, but I also know you can't get better especially with health unless you occasionally test the water. I speak to my guides who reassure me I will make a full recovery, they are working on fine tuning the spiritual connection and in the future, I will never experience this chapter again resulting in ill health.

So what does this mean, why do I feel off-balance, nauseous, dull headed, and on a permanent boat? Why can I connect so well to the spirit world, but then feel so poorly after? Why? What is the point in having all these gifts if that's what you want to call them if I can't use them? I have so many questions and I'm simply told by my spirit guides that I'm being finely tuned, they are nearly there and once completed, I will feel healthy.

I hope so, please let all of this be for a positive, bigger picture to do some good in the world. I constantly remind myself, there are so many people hidden behind closed doors often too poorly physically and mentally to leave the home.

I have experienced this but I've been blessed to have the connection with my spirit guides to reassure me there is a finish line. I sometimes worry for others without loved ones surrounding them, the lonely ones.

This world doesn't give much thought for lonely people and even worse lonely, ill people. We as a species are so consumed by our human rights, working rights, gender rights, prisoner's rights, etc.

I have never heard of the rights of ill health, lonely persons rights, why is this? Because they are hidden away, out of sight for people not to see so therefore not to be given thought or compassion to.

It makes me sad when I think of these people hidden away and often wonder what we could do and more importantly, how we access these people.

There are the brave that ask for help but what about the proud and often too ashamed to ask for help? It's great the times have moved on and people talk about mental ill-health, but how do we get to those people who are struggling the most?

I really don't know what the answer is, but I have sent several thoughts out to the universal law or a higher divine energy to be shown an idea to help. In 2022, I think we should not only be thinking of our human rights, blah, blah, blah, or should I say me, me, me but about others human rights, especially the lonely.

TOO MUCH INFORMATION, PROBABLY

I've already mentioned previously I'm not going to keep harping on about how poorly I feel and the daily strange occurrences of my body being physically moved during meditative states, but I thought this was too cringe-worthy and disturbing not to mention.

It's the 31st of December and I'm reassuring myself how great 2022 is going to be. A new year, new health and how lucky I am to be blessed with so much love surrounding me. I'm trying really hard to feel all of this positivity and upliftment I'm creating with the power of my thoughts.

What is it they say, oh yes, you can manifest anything you want. We create our world with what we perceive as our truth. YEAH RIGHT! I must be really bad at this for I'm feeling like a drunk on a boat with a severe hangover and headache.

I have to remind myself how fortunate I am again. This positive thinking, mind over matter is not only hard, but actually rather annoying and at times rather boring. Whoops, I suddenly forgot what a positive person I am, I must try harder!

It's New Year's Eve, I go to bed sending positive thoughts out for the coming year. I'm in a deep sleep when I become aware I am lying on a surgical table.

Everything is white and sterile. The white of the room is quite startling to the point I am unable to see clearly around the room, yet I know and sense there are lots of beings observing me.

There is the usual familiar doctor with the unruly hair who I know, but I didn't know from somewhere previously.

The interesting thing about this doctor is I know he is the best in advanced scientific technology, including frequency waves and nanotechnology. (Whatever that is?) I also know he is using procedures that haven't been discovered yet but will be in the future.

So how do I know he is male, because his energy feels male. He has smooth, clean, white hands that are smaller than the average man, gentle but strong. His hair looks a little unkempt and that is how I recognise him. I have tried several times to see his face but I am refused permission. Maybe that is a good thing, who knows.

I'm allowed only to see what they want me to see and no more. I'm so at ease in this environment it is literally as though I have been here several times before. I'm not frightened and completely accepting of the situation.

The doctor holds a long, thin, silver surgical probe which has a sharp pointed end. (It looks like a sharp barbeque skew) As the device comes closer, I calmly and unperturbed watch as it is inserted into my right side.

This physically hurts and wakes me up, I feel a little startled and dazed. I have learnt through practise not to start over analysing especially in the middle of the night as I know this will keep me awake. I decide to review what has happened in the morning and drift off back to sleep.

The next morning after having a shower, I first noticed three perfectly uniformed and precise markings on the right side of my stomach. My first response is to simply ignore them, but as the day goes on, I can physically feel discomfort located on the right side.

As I lift up my top to have a look there is a hard lump of tissue where I had dreamt a sharp device had been inserted into my body adjacent to the three small circular bruises that had appeared with exact precision with no explanation. I rack my brain to find an explanation. Perhaps, I pinched myself in the stomach three times whilst using a ruler to get the exact distance.

As a person of little desire of any form of maths, I disregard this immediately. So how could – this happen and how did I create a sore lump of knotted tissue under my skin in the exact location of my dream? I decided there really is no point in over analysing this, for unless I can prove any of this is real, it really doesn't matter.

I console myself with revisiting the dream and asking myself if any of this felt wrong, dark or dangerous. The answer is it all felt safe with good intention. I have learnt over the years to compartmentalise some of the things I have seen, sensed and known, to protect myself from over analysing which amounts to very little good.

I need to offload my concerns, so I confide in Tony. I tell him first about the dream and then I show him the precise markings over my torso. He listens with great intent, but I can see the look of bemusement across his face.

Tony is from an engineering background and so level-headed I almost secretly want him to find an explanation to justify these strange occurrences. I asked him, was I doing anything strange at night.

Tony is a light sleeper so surely he would have noticed if I started pinching or hurting myself. "No, but you did shout out once, as though something had hurt you, but that was it," he said. Well, neither of us could find any reason for these strange markings, so we just changed the conversation.

These conversations are nothing exciting or new, but I do really appreciate that I can talk openly and without being judged. How lucky am I?

I find myself taking a photo, why? I don't know, perhaps to document I'm not making up all of this. A couple of days pass and I'm on the telephone to my lovely friend

Becky and I can't wait to tell her all about my new markings. Becky listens intently and asks to be sent the photo.

I'm reluctant as my stomach doesn't look too pretty at my age, but what the hell if someone can explain this to me then it's worth the risk of my wobbly stomach being leaked!

After reviewing my photo, Becky assured me this was not in my imagination and all of this was very real.

"Becky, what is going on?" I asked. Becky replied, "It is all very real and I can assure you it's not your imagination, but at this point in your life, it really is best you don't know." Now usually I would be like a dog after a bone and wanting to discover and learn more, but the assurance that I wasn't going mad was enough.

I knew this already to be true and I also knew it wouldn't benefit at this precise time on my journey so I agreed with Becky. Some things in life are best left unknown. I'll find out at a later date when I'm more accepting and ready to learn.

After a week or so I couldn't help myself and needed to understand so I sat down and asked my spirit team. I'm informed I am one hundred percent protected and this is not a time to start over analysing. I am to remain focused and write.

ANOTHER RELAXING LIE DOWN

During my daily lie down, as I gently go into my meditative state, I can feel the usual movements within my neck and jaw being gently manipulated. The movements are light and comforting to the point I feel so relaxed I'm actually enjoying the sensation and starting to feel myself dozing off.

I suddenly, out of nowhere, have this impulsive urge to place both my hands on my chin. My hands force my chin back towards my neck resulting in a stomach-churning popping sound and creating a crunching noise in my neck. I feel nauseous, strange and off-balance. I lay there frozen, too scared to move and questioning whether I'll be able to move.

Gingerly, I start by moving my body very slowly until I realise no harm has come to me. I have an unusual sensation in the left side of my chest and my heart begins to flutter. I decided to keep still because I don't feel fully connected in my physical body. I have a clammy cold sensation in the front and back of my head as if fluid within my head is trying to work out how to flow healthily.

After a period of time, I very slowly go down stairs where Tony says, "Jane, are you alright? You look really pale and not really with it." I assure him in front of the kids that I'm fine. When out of the kids' hearing range, I tell him what has just happened. Yikes! That episode I'm not afraid to admit scared the s . . . out of me.

Sometimes, I question why this process is taking so long. I have seen the capability of the healing power on the other side and known their healing techniques are far superior to us humans.

Great! So, why am I not fixed yet? With all that I have experienced, I am not stupid enough not to be able to work out that my physical body probably couldn't withstand the intensity and the vibrational energetic frequency they use. I genuinely believe if this process was rushed, it could kill me.

They on the other side realise we are more than just physical. We are physical, mental, spiritual and emotional beings. There are so many energy layers that surround us. I do not understand any of the science behind what I have just said, but I do know that we as humans are so limited in our healing abilities.

I was just thinking the other day, pharmaceutical companies create wonderful drugs that keep people alive, but very rarely do they produce much that completely heals the body and that one hundred percent guarantees there will be no return of the disease.

Most pharmaceutical drugs suppress symptoms which results in a reliance and continuation of taking drugs. Some drugs cause such awful symptoms the consumer ends up buying more medication to curb the side effects.

A certain heart medication given to millions of people over a certain age causes quite a few side effects for many. The facts are for quite a few million if they perhaps changed their diet and lifestyle, they could eliminate the risks completely.

One disadvantage to this approach, there would be no financial gain. Medication is vital, life-enhancing and life-saving for many but not everyone. I am not anti-medication for we are blessed to live in an era and have access to some of the most advanced medication and superb medical scientists.

I just believe one size doesn't fit all and we as humans can also help ourselves feel a little healthier.

Whoops, I deviated. So as much as I want my health to be better, NOW, I am fully aware my physical body couldn't cope with it. The other thing I have been told is, my physical body must be aligned to my spiritual body. One must not develop quicker than the other. At the beginning of my journey, I could see for myself my spiritual development was developing too quickly.

At the time, I thought it was great as who would not be excited by making progress in a discipline that had been developed over many years. So how can I prevent this from happening to anyone else? The truth is I can't if this is part of your journey also to learn. But you can step away from working spiritually and give your physical body time to rest and catch up. As I have said before, working in such energy is highly addictive so it will require discipline.

You need to respect yourself and have an appreciation of not being able to solve and help everyone. If the physical body becomes ill, you can't help anyone until your health improves.

The hardest lesson I have ever had to learn and one I will not be repeating. If I had known this, would I have behaved any differently? Probably not, looking at my behaviour and personality six and a half years ago, but I would have liked the warning and the knowledge.

DISTURBING DREAM JANUARY 2022

I'm in a hostile war environment. There are several men desperate to show me around a building. It feels like some sort of school. There has recently been a celebration that looks like Christmas decorations, but I have a knowing it is not.

It's a traditional celebration that I don't recognise. Children have lovingly made these decorations and I can sense all the pride, excitement and joy each and every decoration consists of. I see numerous displays of bright coloured pictures and paper decorations hanging from strings across the classroom ceilings.

The men are eager to show me what has happened as if their purpose for living on earth depends on it. I feel uncomfortable but know it is vital I fulfil their cries for help otherwise they will be unable to progress in the spiritual world. The men are traumatised by what they have seen, a strong sense of guilt and anguish for not being able to protect the innocent.

Their pain and hurt makes me feel overwhelmed with a sickening feeling in the pit of my stomach. I'm taken to another classroom and feeling uneasy. The smell of stale blood is so strong I feel I'm about to retch. Bodies of innocent children lay upon the floor drenched in blood. I'm made to look around, absorb what has happened.

It's so important I see and witness what has happened. I vividly remember seeing children cowering in the classroom corners as if somehow that was going to protect them. There are body parts lying upon the classroom floor and I notice a female lady lying lifeless with her arms stretched out as though trying to gather up some of the children.

There are no survivors in the room, but I feel the terror and can hear the cries still present in the air. I need to get out of this dream, I can't for the men insist I need to see everything. They tell me the Western world doesn't know this is going on.

The panic in their voices is tangible. They can not and will not settle until this story has been told. The sadness is heartbreaking, but the feeling of helplessness is unbearable. I'm trying with all my might to get out of the dream, but the energy is almost like a suction that refuses me the choice to leave.

The men repeat I must see what is going on, nobody is aware. The stories and flashing images keep coming. I feel helpless, fatigued and faint by the sights of the grim reality of an inhumane war.

Finally, I woke up! The stench of blood and bodily fluids remains strongly in the air.

I feel an overwhelming sensation to document the dream. I have to write for those men for they will not settle in the spiritual world until I have fulfilled their request.

Why? I don't know.

How can I help those soldiers by writing about their reality? Again, I don't know, but I will honour their request. I don't usually receive information in this way, it's usually in the lighter stage of sleep and I thought I had mastered better control over the outcome.

This dream was not symbolic, this was an insight into the cruelty of this world. It felt like I was using intuition, what do I mean by this? Intuition is knowing where you shouldn't question yourself for you know it to be true.

This dream was not a premonition for unfortunately I knew it had already happened. As much as I tried, this dream kept popping into my thoughts. I couldn't escape the images but more disturbing was the smell of stale blood.

I did the only thing I knew to make myself feel better and that was to send out positive thoughts and found myself praying like the innocent child I used to be, who believed in God and knew he would answer all my prayers and more importantly take away all the pain and suffering especially of those men.

I prayed for those men to find peace in their hearts, but more important for the families who had lost loved ones. I knew the children were in a safe place, loved and being looked after. I needed those men to free themselves from the heartache, guilt and despair so they could continue their spiritual path.

This dream haunted me for several weeks as I had never witnessed anything like it. I felt an empty, dark sadness and worse, a dread physically within that what I had received had some relevance in this world.

With discipline and past experience I could either become consumed with what I had seen or send positive thoughts and love into the world. I chose love!

I had buried this dream in my notebook and only just revealed it today which has immediately taken me back to that horrific scene. I have completed my obligation as I assured those men I would, now I just hope it brings them comfort and healing on the other side.

A JOB INTERVIEW

I've just been speaking to Clarissa who had asked me whether I've contacted the two psychic companies which I reluctantly admit I haven't got around to yet. I confess I don't feel confident and the thought of being tested and failing fills me with dread. "Who is going to find out if you fail, I'm not going to tell anyone," Clarissa said. "You're right, I don't need to tell anyone and I know you can keep a secret," I said.

We start to laugh as I say, "You better not tell anyone if it's discovered I'm a rubbish medium!" Clarissa then says. "Look, first of all you will pass and secondly, you are applying for one of the hardest companies. If she doesn't want you she will have got it wrong and it's her loss."

I start to giggle again at the thought of applying for a psychic job. "Right, Clarissa, no more excuses, as you've said, nobody needs to know, but maybe I'll apply for the second best company as I don't want to put too much pressure on myself." "Jane, just do it, you'll be fine!" said Clarissa.

The following day, I applied for both psychic jobs. I decide whichever company gets back to me first, I will just go for it.

Surprise, surprise, the top psychic company got straight back to me and arranged a test reading.

Shit!

I can feel the panic and anxiety levels hit the roof. I remind myself it doesn't matter as nobody needs to know. I struggle with the idea of being a medium, but don't want to be known as a shitty one! "Breathe, Jane, breathe," I reminded myself.

I send a thought to my guides that they better step in quickly when I get tested. I'm reassured by my guides everything will be fine. The stress of waiting for that telephone call to be put to the test is unbearable. I discovered just how pathetic I am at dealing with stress.

I'm constantly in the toilet and then pacing up and down. The phone rings, yikes! My voice is trembling as I speak to the operator. Now as a psychic tarot card reader is aware, it is so much easier to read for someone if they have a question or an area of their life to look at.

One direction or word whether that be looking at their work, family, or lovelife just allows the cards to flow.

Once the flow begins, my guides step in and basically take over. I ask the operator if there is any aspect of her life she would like me to look at. She immediately replies, "NO!

A general reading please." This is much harder so off I go and the flow is let's say much to my horror not flowing. I get further down the reading and it's going terribly.

My guides step in where I suddenly say, "I'm being told there is one question you want to ask me." Silence!

Which feels like eternity. The operator says "That's funny, a question has just popped into my head." Thank the Lord, I'm back in the game.

The reading is flowing and my guides are so close it's reassuring. The operator says thank you and puts the phone down.

So what happens now, how did I do?

I started to analyse my performance, it was okay but certainly not my best. The phone rings again and I am informed I have got to the next stage and I will have another test the following day.

As I'm sitting there already dreading the next test, I reflect on all the stress I have inflicted unnecessarily on myself.

This is ridiculous how much stress I am subjecting myself to. I'm going to chill out as best as I can tomorrow for at least I know what to expect. Here we go again I'm pacing up and down the hallway telling myself what will be, will be and just to do my best.

Yikes!

My heart drops as the phone rings. A different person

comes onto the phone, but this time I feel calmer. The reading was fascinating, diverse and I've never had to work so hard.

This person certainly knew how to stretch every aspect of the psychic. Once again, there is no feedback and the phone is put down. I'm happy with the reading I have just done. It was my best so if they don't want me, then I accept my defeat with grace.

The phone rings back again which makes me jump out of my skin. I am told by the operator the owner who is a celebrity within her own rights will be ringing me shortly for a reading.

Bloody hell, I wasn't expecting to be tested by her!

The phone rings and I'm greeted by the owner. She is professional and friendly, but you have the sense immediately she is here to exchange business. I ask her if there is any area of her life she would like me to look at. "No, just general," she replies.

Great, this is going to be tough, but as soon as I thought that, I felt the strong presence of my guides. All fear melted away as I began the reading and blended with my team. Halfway through, she told me to stop, which made me question if I had done something wrong.

She said, "You have the job, that is one of the best readings I have ever had. Not even my experienced psychic readers are able to pick up what you have just picked up." I sighed a breath of relief.

The owner then asked me if I would read for her, but this time she asked me a question which will always remain confidential.

The question was answered with a blend of the cards and with the help of my spiritual team and she seemed happy with the reading.

She also reiterated that I was to congratulate myself as she only took one out of every two hundred applicants as she couldn't afford for anyone to lower the standard of her company. (I'm still not a hundred percent convinced, but I'll take the compliment.)

Whilst reading for this lovely, warm and interesting lady, I could feel all the pressure of continual expectations on her. When you are known as one of the best in the field, it comes with such constant pressure.

I decided there and then all those famous successful people could keep their status for it felt energetically more of a burden than an enjoyment.

The beauty of this job was I could keep my identity concealed, I didn't want to be put on a pedestal always anticipating someone trying to knock me off. To be honest, it was stressful enough just being tested.

I messaged Tony as I knew he was in a meeting with my good news before rushing to tell Clarissa all the juicy gossip. "Well done, Jane! You do realise what you have just done?" said Clarissa. "What do you mean?" I said. "Jane, she is one of the toughest people to pass a test with, she is renowned for being incredibly hard to impress, for she only takes the best.

She only takes one out of two hundred applicants and can't afford for anyone to let her company down. You must explain to Tony how well you have done because he won't appreciate or get it," Clarissa said. "Well, now you tell me, why didn't you tell me all of this before?"

Clarissa started to chuckle, "Because I knew you wouldn't have gone for it!" We both burst out laughing and I assured her I wouldn't have gone for it if I had known the whole truth. I asked Clarissa if she would have gone for it, which she replied. "No way! I wouldn't be good enough." We both burst out laughing again before I became serious and said, "Clarissa, you are one of the best mediums I know and she would not only be lucky but privileged to have someone like you work for her." I could hear Clarissa start to laugh again as she repeated, she would not be subjecting herself through that ordeal.

That evening, I got a telephone call from my friend Gareth, who is also a talented psychic/medium. "Just felt like I needed to speak to you as you have been on my mind," he said. I told Gareth I was continuing with my writing, but had just got a job for a certain company.

He seemed impressed. "Jane, are you sure you want to do this for it will take all of your energy and you are not fully recovered yet?" asked Gareth. I assured him it would be fine as although I was still working with my spirit guides, it was an easier energy to work in.

I can blend in and out of psychic energies which are less demanding on the body than being used solely as a medium where the intensity and strength of being used basically as a vessel is a lot more demanding. Gareth wished me well but warned me the way I worked was quite extreme and to be aware of looking after my energy.

The last words I said were, "I'll be fine. Anyway, it will be something to tell the grandchildren."

I'M A WORKING WOMAN

I have to say the company was very professional. A strict code of conduct and the telephone operators were lovely ladies making me feel immediately part of the team.

The first day I really enjoyed it but noticed my energy was depleting too quickly. I pushed myself through then found myself sitting on the couch feeling drained, nauseous and pale. I knew I wasn't fully well, but I hadn't been expecting to feel this fatigued.

Each time a new person rang, I could immediately feel how they were feeling and the turmoil in their lives. I am a perfectionist so every reading had to be to a high standard. I used the cards as an aid whilst blending and listening to my guides, this was not a problem.

The problem was picking up all the heightened energy of the humans. The senses, emotions and heightened anxiety in some of the people was so tiring. I could literally feel the life draining from me. I confided in Tony.

He asked me why I felt the need to do this and had nothing to prove to anyone and certainly not myself. "Jane, I'm scared for your health, it has taken us years to get you to this point. We can't afford to go backwards. We don't need the money so please really think seriously about what you are doing.

This could affect the whole family and we have been through enough. The girls have only just got their mother back." I wasn't expecting that brutal honesty but that is one thing I can always guarantee with Tony, the truth!

I thought about it long and hard and decided to give it another go. Again, after a couple of hours, I felt awful. I found myself lying on the couch not knowing what to do with myself as I felt so sick. My energy just didn't like working this way for prolonged periods.

I didn't say anything to Tony as I didn't want to make him worry. I went to bed early, the thought of doing more readings filled me with dread which I had never experienced before. I woke up in the early hours of the morning with the room spinning.

I lay there frozen reassuring myself this would eventually pass, which thankfully it did. All the memories of my past health battles came flashing back. Memories of being so ill, unable to leave the house, due to dizziness and vertigo attacks.

The guilt of not being able to take my children to after school clubs and the reality of how if I didn't look after my health just how miserable my life was to become. I made a decision, I would ring the company tomorrow. I rang the company and told them the truth about how I had suffered with a previous illness and thought I was not well enough to work.

The company was great and said I could literally work whatever hours I wanted as they wanted to keep me. My guides drew in closely and I knew exactly what I had to do. I told the company I could no longer work for them for my health was more important.

The lady said she would keep my details and if I ever wanted to work for them again, I would be very welcome. I had made the right decision as it took a further two weeks for my health to make a full recovery.

I sat down two weeks later and asked my guides why they had allowed me to do that. Their answer was that I don't always listen and had to learn for myself. The spirit world wanted me to write, nothing else, just WRITE!

I have to admit the harsh reality was, I wasn't well enough to work for others yet which was frustrating but true.

My physical and spiritual bodies were still being finely tuned for what? We will have to wait and see. I had been told by my guides several times all they wanted from me was to write.

There are many talented psychic/mediums out there to do readings but that wasn't the plan for me at the present time. I needed to be used as a channel for writing and to tell my cringe-worthy story. So it was back once again to the computer. I can't express how much I prefer practical activities and writing really isn't one of them. I also know this journey has already been written and my guides know the final outcome. I think I'll give it a go and start listening to my guides, but properly this time.

ACCEPTANCE WITH WAVES OF FRUSTRATION

Right, I've learnt the hard way so now I know what I have to do. I must accept my path and wait for my spiritual team to finish off perfecting our connection, finely tune me and BINGO!

I'll finally feel like a new woman! I've finally got it, the penny has dropped, shut up, Jane, accept your fate and wait patiently.

So, I wait patiently and continue to write this book. I find writing which you can probably tell by my lack of descriptive writing and finesse really hard. I really don't understand why the spirit world chose me of all the things to do, write.

I also know from experience they know what they are doing so I shall just continue to write in my own limited style. Life is good. I'm constantly grateful for what I have and how far I have come.

Sometimes, I will admit I have doubts that perhaps I am delusional and perhaps this is as good as it gets. I then quickly have a strong word with myself and focus on what I have been told by my guides. My spiritual guides only speak words of truth which at times can be harsh, but also comforting.

Certain family members look at me with pity in their

eyes when I reassure them it won't be long now for my health to improve. I get it, it sounds a little desperate and perhaps fictitious, we'll see who is right! Please let it be me!

The healing sessions continue, each day I allocate a set time to lie down and receive healing from my divine healers. Each healing session I look at with fascination, positivity and gratitude although at times I do become fearful and have to remind myself I'm in safe hands.

In March 2022, whilst in a deep meditative state, the right side of my head was moved and made a horrific clonking sound of bone grinding against bone. The ligaments and structures in my face were aggressively forced with the sensation of facial tissues being almost torn and you could feel and hear the tissues being realigned.

My facial muscles locked and I was completely unable to move my face and was too scared to try. I lay there, stomach turning with nausea and fear. I knew I had to completely relax and succumb to the process for my guide's presence was strong, reassuring me I was protected and no harm or danger would occur.

Within what seemed like a lifetime, my facial muscles returned to normal. After this occurrence, my left shoulder and scapular felt like it had dropped.

I was wondering whether to mention this to my massage therapist as I was still going for regular massages, but I decided it would sound completely crazy and far-fetched. I had previously implied I had been experiencing manipulations through my body but didn't want to over emphasis the situation.

I'm not completely stupid and appreciate how ridiculous it sounds to the average person – all these strange physical occurrences. The massage therapist I see is very open-minded and spiritually gifted, but I remind myself how I would have reacted six years ago if I had been told this.

I know I wouldn't have judged, but would have certainly sat on the fence and probably not been convinced either way. I make the decision not to mention anything unless she picks up any postural changes herself and if she does, I'll tell her at the end.

Whilst having a deep tissue massage which isn't very relaxing she comments on how tight the right side of my upper body is. She also mentions the left side feels like it has dropped. Hallelujah! I'm not making up all of this. I know what the truth is but it really does bring comfort when your truth is given confirmation.

At the end of the massage, she places her hands on either side of my face. I'm feeling so relaxed as I know the massage is coming to an end. My eyes start to flicker out of control. No! No! No! I cannot and will not let this happen in front of another person. I'm so tired and have this pleasant sensation of warmth embracing my body as though I'm being cradled in a layer of love and protection.

The room feels intense but strangely calm and comforting. I feel overwhelmed to let go and hand myself over to the process. My eyes are now flickering completely out of control. My head is moved bolt upright and my jaw is moved into strange end range positions.

The jaw has been forced into an end range position releasing the neck which fills the air with strange cracking and popping sounds which are literally coming from my upper body. As I lay there, energy is being released from within my body and energy is flowing down the right side of my torso.

The process of physical manipulation continues and all the time the massage therapist calmly and reassuringly keeps her hands at either side of my head and doesn't bat an eyelid. This woman has got serious balls as in my younger days I would have been straight out of the door!

Eventually, the process comes to an end. I feel calm and as though it was the right thing to do. I also feel a little amused by sharing this process and concerned it might have been too much for the massage therapist. I say to her, "I hope you are okay with what you have just witnessed?

That is what has been occurring when I mentioned the

spirit world have been working on me." The massage therapist seems calm and accepting of what she has just seen and says, "Fascinating, you are gifted and have been chosen for something." I keep repeating, "Are you sure you are okay with what has just happened? "You do know I wasn't doing that by myself," I said.

The massage therapist confirms. "Oh yes, I know that wasn't you for you couldn't move your body in those positions and manipulate your spine with such precision. That was coming from a higher spiritual level, fascinating, so gifted!"

Gifted I thought, what interesting words to describe what had just taken place. We sat down and had a really frank, honest and open conversation.

I had nowhere to hide after that and also I didn't want to. I felt a mixture of relief that someone had finally witnessed my hidden secret, but also a concern that I hadn't frightened the hell out of her.

She reassured me she was fine and found it all fascinating, but I also knew she would need time to reflect on what the heck had just happened. I reassured her it was an honour that I had trusted her enough to relax and allow the process to happen for I had never allowed anyone to witness my channelled healing sessions.

She thanked me and assured me it was an honour. I knew her words to be true and believed her for her truth, honesty and love shone through. I have to admit for the next couple of weeks I kept having moments of feeling mortified and embarrassed.

Someone had witnessed what looked like something out of a horror movie. That poor lady, I just hoped it wasn't too much for her. I also knew deep within she needed to witness that for in the future, she, although unaware at the moment, would be developing her own healing abilities.

SHAMANIC HEALING

On a previous mediumship workshop, I met a healer who implied I needed healing, for my energy really shouldn't be depleting so quickly whilst I was working. I told her I had tried a variety of healing sessions on numerous occasions, but each time there had been no significant improvement.

I assured her I had even found the best. "What do you mean the best?" she asked. I had discovered or been led to a gifted lady who was actually in her earlier days a qualified neurologist so an intelligent woman who wasn't as many presume away with the fairies.

Literally, when she touched your body you could physically feel the energy run through your body like a pleasant warm form of energy running from her hands through your entire body. I would leave her healing session feeling optimistic, my cheeks would be rosy and I would feel full of energy and hope.

I saw this lady for months full of optimism, but unfortunately it wasn't my time to heal. This lady healed people who scientifically couldn't be healed.

She treated fellow medical consultants who were in pain and highly respected people who worked in the medical field. The funny thing is not one of them was brave enough to recommend her to the world.

Yes, secretly to maybe fellow friends but not to society. How would this appear on them, associating themselves with what some would call a charlatan!

A woman who could take away pain and heal with no pharmaceutical drugs. The years of education these medical consultants had studied and yet no scientific explanation of how this lady could reduce their pain.

The joke of it all was she was originally one of them so they couldn't ridicule her for she was held in great esteem. She was the real deal for you could physically feel an electrical warm current running throughout your body and you felt great afterwards.

We were chatting whilst she was healing me and she said the strangest thing, "I wonder sometimes if the reason you are here is for me to give you my healing ability." She said that quite flippantly, but I remembered her words and found it quite strange.

This lady was also so highly intelligent she moved quickly from one statement to another. I suppose if you have studied as a neurologist you are going to be perhaps a little less conventional than the norm.

This is a compliment if any neurologists are reading this book, basically highly intelligent!

She was a little eccentric, but in a warm, loving and very endearing way.

She was also full of energy, a lover of life and I would dare to say energised each time she gave healing. A fascinating character who had also experienced hard times throughout her life so she really had got the full package of gifts, empathy, sympathy and previous hardships.

I was sad when naturally our time came to an end, but I also knew for some reason my progress was on a timeline and would only be complete at exactly the right time.

My family was annoyed that I had seen this lady for such a long period of time. Out of protection, they thought she was a fake but I assured them this lady was a true, gifted healer she just wasn't permitted to heal me physically.

My family couldn't understand why I wasn't cross with the false hope of complete healing. What most people aren't aware of is that when you work as a true healer, not someone who has just completed a couple of courses online, the spirit world uses you as a channel and gives you access to what that person needs at the time.

The healer might think they are healing, but really they are just being used as a channel. That explains why some people heal and others take longer.

No healer can guarantee the perfect outcome and if they do I would suggest they have allowed their ego to take over and forgotten who is really in charge of the healing process.

As a true healer, you can't heal without a divine energy or team of spirit guides. You can choose to believe whatever makes you feel most comfortable, but the reality is it all comes from a spiritual divine source.

The healer I had met at the mediumship workshop said, "Have you ever thought about a shamanic healer for if you find the right one they have the ability to remove energies that have attached to people over the years?"

She mentioned she saw a shamanic healer every few months to ensure other people's energies didn't fatigue hers. Especially in her choice of work as a Reiki massage practitioner. At the time of the conversation I thought, "Yeah, I've heard this all before, I'm not convinced and what the bloody hell is a shaman healer?"

Those words for some reason kept popping into my head. I decided to research what a shaman healer was. For those of you who don't know, shaman healing is the oldest of all spiritual healing, it's thousands of years old. A shaman healer works in a trance state journeying to other invisible worlds where they work with spirit, including animal spirits.

Shamans heal by returning lost parts of a soul due to perhaps a past trauma. They have the ability to cleanse the body and remove dark, negative energy that are preventing the body, mind or spirit from healing. There is obviously a lot more to shaman healing than this simple explanation so if you are interested it might be worth having a quick google.

I also kept getting this feeling something could be attached to me, but surely not? As I have said before I really don't like to analyse other topics like attachments, paranormal activities, entities, ghosts etc. I'm happy with the gifts I've got and when the time is right,

I'll use them to help others, but I need to keep my world as simple as possible. I like to think of myself as grounded and relatable. I decide to push these feelings away, but then I keep getting images of a person I knew a few years ago just before I started getting sick. Again and again I see his face being shown to me.

Michael was a guy I met at the gym. To keep it short Michael is gifted spiritually and removes dark energies for example haunted houses that others have failed at. I don't fully understand what other work he does but he is surrounded by powerful guides that eliminate dark forces.

That's as much as I want to know. Originally, I didn't know this about Michael, but every time I saw or felt his presence, I felt overcome with nausea, heightened awareness to protect myself and a sense of intrigue. I would find myself trying to move myself as far away as possible from him.

Whilst in the gym changing room, I asked the other ladies basically what they knew about this intense character. Straight away I was filled in with all the gossip of this ghostbuster, haunted house eliminator and fascinating character.

No wonder I felt horrified to be in his presence. We worked at complete opposites of the spectrum when it came to the spirit world. My work was pure, loving, light and healing.

His work was to dabble with darkness and eliminate it.

The problem with working with darkness is, I suspect, this is more of an inner knowing, to be really good at eliminating evil/darkness at some point in a previous life you would have done evil. (I have absolutely no proof of this!)

My guides told me I needed to help him. How the hell was I supposed to help a person who kicked the arse of evil spirits? Really! I think that is even for me a little bit sick and twisted for I couldn't cope with the strength and dark energy surrounding him.

As time passed, I learnt very quickly to sense his presence in the gym and would start protecting myself. I won't lie, I felt fear but also knew I had to get a grip as I also knew fear weakens your strength and would make me more vulnerable.

I felt my guides surround me and reassure me I was just

as powerful and had complete control. Yikes! I even thought about leaving the gym as I felt out of my depth.

As the weeks passed, I had perfected my protection and self belief, but more importantly, I had perfected my skills at keeping my distance.

Sat in the jacuzzi with several other people, suddenly Michael appears from nowhere. I felt a rush of horror and panic flow through my veins. Within seconds it had gone from an overcrowded jacuzzi to just me and him staring at each other.

We started talking, I don't know exactly what I said as spirit literally took over, but I do know the words made him stop, think about his life and reminded him of his true inner, pure self.

Right healing done, I need to get out of here! Michael was naturally a pure light, but working constantly in dark energy had taken its toll.

You might have gathered by now I don't reveal other people's journeys and not about to reveal how Michael had been affected, for that's his private business.

So why now did I keep getting images of his face, surely not! I have this strange feeling in my stomach and a knowing that perhaps some of Michael's energy might have attached itself to me.

I sat down and asked the spirit, "Do I need to see a

shaman healer?" The answer is yes, really you know I'm not into all of that stuff. I'm told I need to see a specific healer who will have the ability to let my spirit team use her as a channel.

So, where the hell am I going to find a proper shaman healer? Let's be honest, if you look on the internet, it's pretty frightening as well as a little amusing at the variety of people who call themselves shamans.

I suddenly remember seeing drumming equipment and asking questions at a practice that offered holistic treatments. I'm sure someone there did shamanic healing. I researched it and the shamanic healer's face popped up.

She looked normal, I didn't feel any negativity from her photo so I asked my team what they thought. They confirmed this lady had the ability and the healing capacity to help me. I have to admit I questioned my spiritual team several times for I had been down the healing route before and it had made very little difference.

"Jane, she has the ability and we will be able to use her as a channel to help you," they told me. Reluctantly, I agreed as to be honest, I wasn't sure about the whole shamanic healing world, but I also knew it felt right and had been assured several times by my guides I was hundred percent protected and no harm would come to me.

I booked a shamanic healing session, still not convinced, but I comfort myself with the fact, at least I am protected. The day of my healing treatment arrives, I haven't got a clue what to expect, but I have a little giggle to myself about how I have ended up with a shaman. You really couldn't make this stuff up!

I'm greeted by a pleasant normal-looking woman, by this I mean she isn't dressed up in any strange gear with hundreds of crystals hanging off her. (Not that there's anything wrong with this!) She is warm, friendly and immediately puts me at ease.

I immediately pick up that her energy is pure, she is gifted and she has had a demanding and hard journey of her own.

The experiences she has endured have heightened her ability to heal, but not only that but have made her incredibly compassionate, wise and knowledgeable. I have to remind myself to stop reading her for I'm here to be healed.

The session begins with a conversation on identifying the different ages I was when I experienced traumatic times in my life. Surprise, surprise, these experiences affect you physically, mentally, emotionally and spiritually.

Now I'm not about to declare my deepest darkest secrets but as everyone else I have rather a few traumas and bumps along my path. Rather a lot in my younger days which I had forgotten about.

Next thing is I'm asked to lie on the couch, just before we are about to begin, she asks me to stop reading her for I am here to relax not work. Whoops, I don't even realise I'm doing it at times. I'm already impressed she has picked this up.

Immediately she is drawn and mentions a previous life of mine. What do I mean by a previous life? Some people choose to believe we have lived several lives, before we come back down to earth. Certain religions believe in this and certain religions forbid us to think in this way.

I was brought up in a religion strongly against this belief so naturally I had always stirred away from the thought of previous lives. In my younger days, I chose to bury my head in the sand and respect others' beliefs, but just found this knowledge too much to get my head around.

I'm a great fan of not over complicating life and dealing with what is in front of you. At the time, I was coping with accepting myself as a medium so this was put on the back burner. I've never felt the desire to explore past lives, but during healing sessions and spiritual workshops I have also seen myself in past lives.

When you see yourself in a past life, not only do you see but you sense, smell and live in that very moment in that past life.

At the time of visiting a past life, it becomes more real than the present moment. (Get your head around that one!)

I have no doubt that we all have lived several times before but I keep this view quiet so as not to offend anyone, especially those with certain religious beliefs. The previous life the shaman picks up is one I have already visited, felt and seen.

She mentions I was a female slave in the Egyptian times. I had been chained, beaten and abused in horrific ways. I had seen this life several times not only in regressions but also in my dreams (not the abuse, thankfully). For months, I went through a period of waking up checking my wrists for chains. I always felt so relieved when I came out of a dream to the current time to see my hands were free.

The sensation and smell of rusty metal devices around my wrists was so real, I could feel the weight, the discomfort and heaviness of them. I would find this very unsettling, but just kept quiet and got on with life (Let's face it, some things are better not shared). Wait for it, it gets better!

The shaman then mentioned at some stage, they had aggressively ripped my tongue out. I suddenly felt overwhelmed knowing all of this past life regression was true for I had been physically woken in the night with my tongue being manipulated or healed?

The connections were all starting to synchronise. She went on to explain that in that era I would have been forced to sign a contract, signing myself over to the master. Apparently, by signing myself over that was for life/eternity so the first thing we had to do was go back and visit those times.

It was eerie how easy it was for me to step straight back into that time. The heat was stifling, the air dry and the land dusty and barren. There was no mistaking I had been there before for everything was so familiar. I visualised the contract I had signed, eager to see what my name was, but quickly realised I couldn't write and had left a simple mark. As I tore the contract up and threw it in the fire, I felt immediately liberated and lighter.

As I'm lying there on the couch, I start to see flashes of Michael's face. I'm thinking this really isn't the time to go off such a significant moment.

I feel the urge to mention him. I say, "I might be being silly, but I have this strange feeling something is attached to the bottom of my spine and is wrapped around my spine which is causing my body to feel off balance. I also have a feeling it has come from a man called Michael that I met at the gym." She immediately describes Michael in great detail and says she knows him and this has happened to many women before. "Did he touch you on your back?" she asked. I replied I can't remember at any point Michael making any physical contact with me, but I also knew his guides could have without Michael even being aware.

I explained that once whilst knowing Michael I had been visited by his spiritual team who I thought at the time had given me healing. The strength of his guides was so powerful it literally knocked me off my feet.

The power of the connection to my head was physically painful. An instant blow to the side of the head as though I had been kicked in the temple by a horse. As soon as the pain made contact, it quickly vanished making me feel physically sick.

The immediate moment after what I had perceived as healing I had absolutely no pain anywhere in my body. It was blissful and how I would imagine a miracle to feel. Unfortunately, it only lasted a few minutes, but I was genuinely left speechless. I have never experienced such power, strength, pain and relief of pain all in one moment.

When I thanked Michael for his healing, he refused to believe me for he had not given permission and certainly hadn't sent me healing. He shortly came back a few minutes later to clarify his guides had given me healing, but he was not aware of this at the time.

I believed him for he offered me healing at a friend's discount, but I politely declined because all of this as much as intriguing didn't feel right.

Michael looked confused and a little annoyed that his team had given away energy without his knowing.

The shaman then said, "Jane, all of your symptoms make perfect sense, I need to put an invisible cloak over what we are doing for Michael is powerful and will know what we are doing." Yikes! This really is stretching my comfort zone.

I decided to keep my eyes closed as I'm not convinced I want to see anymore. This is a little stupid as I see everything very clearly in my mind's eye. After a while she asks me how I feel, thinking everything has been removed, but I tell her there is something still hiding in my back.

I don't know what it is, but I sense it and my guides push me to be strong and tell her it's still there. The shaman starts to look deeper into my back and finds it.

She explains it looks like a fetus with several legs and is entwined and has been growing up my spine. It was already there before I met Michael but he has added to it. I'm struggling with what I have just heard when I feel the presence of my guides surround me. I feel hands on either side of my shoulders reassuring me I am totally safe and I need to relax.

I feel a gentle sensation in my back and a feeling of relief. I have a huge smile across my face which I can't control as my guides step in closer and I feel the safety not only off their strength and protection, but also their love.

As I lie there enjoying the sensation, I see the trunk of a very old tree grow up out of my shoulders into my neck and as it reaches the base of my skull, it blossoms into a beautiful blossom tree of a variety of pinks, lilacs and colours that haven't been discovered or can be named.

The branches and blossoms on this tree explode into the room and I feel overwhelmed by a wave of euphoria, joy and gratitude running through my entire body.

Finally, I feel free.

 I don't understand what has just happened but I feel light, happy, my true self and most importantly, a sense of freedom.

Until this experience, I hadn't noticed or realised how encaged and imprisoned I had felt. The sensation and gratitude in my heart is humbled yet at the same time empowered.

I know this is just the beginning of my journey, I have been taught I am in control and finally free to complete whatever it is in this lifetime.

I was sceptical about this healing session but bloody hell that was amazing!

At the end of the session, we confirm what each of us saw and witnessed. It is liberating to be able to speak so honestly and openly to a fellow lightworker and confirms you aren't just making ridiculous stories up.

You know you aren't, but it really is wonderful to be able to share your experience with a like-minded person.

I'm a little dumbstruck because I need time to process what has just taken place. I still choose to think of Michael as part of my schooling for he has given me a wealth of knowledge. I also choose to believe it was his spirit team and he is genuinely unaware of the decisions his team made that day.

Call me naive, even stupid, but the day I give up seeing love and light in people then I have truly lost my way. I have seen the light in Michael's soul and it is bright.

I will not ever again be naive to the strength of the spirit world and I'm on a quest to protect myself from not ever having to experience anything like that again. It was the shaman that suggested I needed to up my game with protection especially when working within the spiritual realms.

She was quite shocked how little I had been protecting my energy. When helping others it would make sense that your energy, if you allowed it, would become depleted and that was exactly unbeknown to me what I had been doing. No more, I was on a mission to learn and do everything to protect my energy.

As I left the healing room I also knew I would have to revisit for I still hadn't dealt with past trauma at certain ages of life and I was now desperate to move forwards and had finally found a gifted lady that could help me unlock those doors.

The next few days I feel strange, my neck and head feel freer and more balanced, but my pelvis feels really unstable almost as though it could crumble. I just put this down to if you have had an alien, entity, weird thing with legs removed from your body, you are probably going to feel off balance.

I start to giggle as I realise what I have just thought and how stranger my life becomes the more accepting of it I become.

It's a bank holiday, we have managed to get a short break to Hayling Island. Whilst having a family walk down the beach I suddenly experience horrific, severe, sharp pain in my pelvis that takes my breath away. Tony turns around and asks me if I'm okay as I have gone white. I'm frightened because I haven't felt pain like this since my late twenties when I struggled to walk due to previous injuries.

All the memories and fears come flashing back. I don't want to and can't go back to that chapter of my life.

Basically, keep the story short, in my late twenties for several years I struggled to walk due to pain. I have learnt over the years to manage my daily pain and have learnt what activities make things worse and also how to adapt.

Very few people know I have injuries for I choose not to be defined by them. I also cringe and feel uncomfortable when I hear myself verbalise them aloud. I can't bear the thought of becoming a victim. I know counsellors would give me a name for this and I should deal with it, but I think I have enough going on at the moment.

Funny how professionals like to label people, I'm not really into labels. Never allow another to label you unless you want to be labelled (Just my opinion!).

The pain is so severe I need to sit down but where? I see some local toilets. I'm trying to disguise the pain and feel like I'm going to project vomit. Thankfully, the younger two are oblivious but my eldest child notices. "Are you okay, mum?" asked my eldest.

I reassure her I am fine and just have a little bit of discomfort in my pelvis. "You're not pregnant, are you?" I snapped and told her that's not what you want to hear when you are feeling poorly.

Happy family day out! Kids are so funny and say the most inappropriate things at exactly the wrong time. I immediately apologised for the pain had made me overreact.

The next couple of days, I have to take it gently. I use

the dog as an excuse to stay in the holiday home so the others can go shopping without us. I'm not ruining my kid's holiday and I don't want them worrying.

I'm scared for those past memories of being confined to very little quality of life come flooding back.

I know from experience not to push through it, take the painkillers and listen to my body. I also know I need to go back to the Shaman as soon as possible for I have opened up a can of worms and the process hasn't been finished.

I now start to question whether I should have just left things alone and been thankful for the quality of life I had. Too late now, I'm committed.

IN FOR A PENNY, IN FOR A POUND

As soon as we get home, I arrange another shamanic healing session. I know what to expect so I start to log down all the ages when I experienced further traumas in my life. Without going into all my private life, I am comfortable to reveal that from the age of twenty eight to thirty seven, I had six pregnancies.

Three babies survived and three babies weren't quite ready for this world. The three pregnancies that weren't ready for this world ended up in being rushed to hospital and being surgically removed. I found this period of my life not only challenging, but absolutely heartbreaking and devastating.

To this day the only thing that reduces me to tears is the loss of those pregnancies. I'm currently doing that ugly face crying, snotty thing!

For any lady who has experienced the loss of a pregnancy, I just want to say, "I am deeply sorry for your loss."

So my logical brain says hopefully once the shamanic healer has healed these traumas I should be healed, right?

I'm sitting outside the healing room looking forward to moving my life forwards. As the shaman calls me in, I notice the room is very cold and feels like a cold frosty early morning when the ice is still frozen upon the car windows. I'm polite and decide not to mention this.

The energy in the room also feels heightened and very intense. I can't work out whether I like it or not, but it feels safe. We discuss the ages of my challenges throughout life, but then she quickly says she feels the energy in the room is full of strong energy and knows my guides will be doing most of the healing today using her the shaman as their channel.

She also asks whether I have noticed a tall lady dressed in white standing in the corner and if I know her. I reply I haven't seen her. I lie on the couch and relax. I quickly feel my guides draw in and feel the touch of my Indian guide upon my left shoulder which instantly fills me with a sense of safety and trust.

I then see the lady to my right who is dressed in some sort of white robe holding a staff with some sort of round ball on top. She is taller than the room and has a higher vibration. She is shaking as though it is difficult for her to be present and work at this lower energy level. I try to see her face but I'm refused access. I'm told by my guides to stop working and go with the procedure, I have to succumb to this moment and trust.

I decide it's probably better just to go with it as I know if they want me to see anything, they will show me. As I'm lying there, I feel overwhelmed with a sense of peace, total belonging and love. I saw my Indian guide with such clarity and stood behind him a tribe of Indians stood in overgrown wild grass.

There seems to be hundreds of them and I know they all know me and I know each and every one of them. I feel tearful because it feels like I have come home. It's almost like I have spent thousands of years fighting through lifetimes feeling incomplete looking and searching for something that belongs to me.

They have finally found me and I have finally found them. My heart feels like it is singing. I know what and who I am. This is the first time in my life where I have felt that I actually fit in and belong. I want to leave this body and be with them.

The shaman picks up that I'm not grounded and starts doing rituals to ensure I remain in my body. I feel grounded but still have this strong desire to be with my tribe. As the healing continues, I experience flashbacks of me being a blond haired, blue-eyed, perfectly modified and engineered male soldier. I'm trying to escape because I refuse to be used any longer for warfare and corruption I do not agree with.

The other soldiers are compliant and programmed to perfection, super soldiers, like clones of a manufactured scientific experiment. Something has failed in my programming for I will not fully conform and know what is right and wrong.

I continue to try and escape but I can't see the final

outcome. As I'm seeing this my face is being adjusted, my jaw forced to end range position and my eyes flickering out of control. My shoulders are elevated and my head is rotating forwards and backwards. It feels as though they are trying to dislocate my jaw to realign it.

The physical movements in my body calm down and I see standing in front of me another Indian, but this one, I don't seem to know. His eyes are a gentle, wise, deep brown which then change into two piercing red laser lights. I have seen this before and know this being is from a higher vibration and of higher superior intelligence.

This being is safe and of good intention. How do I know, I just do. His eyes return to brown for he has already identified his true self. He offers me his hands which without questioning, I take. He gently lifts me up and out of my body.

I am still aware part of me is in my physical body, but I'm now also standing by his side observing myself lying on the couch.

Why has this just happened, I genuinely don't know yet but also know it will all become apparent. It feels like the process is working its way through layers of my body. I'm guided gently back into my body desperately trying not to start analysing what has just happened so I go back into a meditative state.

My face starts becoming distorted again being put into

strange positions and suddenly I feel this device or metal plate inside the left side of my head and face being removed and going towards the white lady who is struggling to work in this energy and is shaking uncontrollably which I presume is causing the temperature to drop in the room.

I feel so excited that finally this thing has been removed from my face. I feel so overwhelmed by the whole journey and the feeling of completion I can't hold back the tears. Tears are streaming down my face for the gratitude I feel is so humbling and beautiful.

As soon as I've had the experience, literally within seconds I feel the device being put back on my face. Before I have time to process, the shaman mentions something about a bear spirit entering the room which as you can imagine diverts my attention. I can't see a bear, but I do feel a large presence which feels powerful, strong, but also comfortingly gentle.

I have a little chuckle to myself as to the words that are so freely spoken in the room. I'm lying there feeling completely at peace with the situation. The shaman then says, "Snake has just appeared and is by my side," which I must admit isn't the first spirit animal I would have chosen. I remind myself this is not a time to start thinking, just accept the process.

I'm desperate to move forward with my health, so bring it on! As soon as I return to a relaxed state the shaman says, "Snake is entering into your body." Yikes! It's only a spirit snake I justify to myself. The shaman then explains that the snake is clearing up past lives and energies that have hindered my development.

As I'm lying there, I feel overwhelmed by a pleasant feeling of warmth followed by a strange sensation that my blood feels like millions of tiny bubbles but being cleaned up. The sensation moves around my body including my arms, chest and head.

When the movement starts in my head, I feel off balance and nauseous. The snake spirit senses this and moves into my stomach area where I'm feeling this pleasant tingling and bubbling sensation.

The whole experience feels pleasant and pure. I repeatedly feel waves of euphoria, happiness and love as though the more the snake cleans my body up of past disruption, the lighter and purer channel I become.

I also have to mention all of these experiences feel so familiar and aren't concerning me at all, how and when did I become so accepting of spirit animals! This is the first time in my life I have total knowing, trust and acceptance.

The shaman says, "That's unusual, Snake is staying with you and is in your stomach area at the moment." The shaman uses the drums around my feet as she needs to remove something. I have sensory problems and hate most noises but I love these drums. Again, the sound of the drums fills my body with a familiar sense of comfort and reassurance. The drums vibrate across my feet which is rather pleasant as I feel the heavy weight removed almost like a heavy pair of metal boots. The shaman asked, "Where is all of this going?"

I'm feeling fatigued especially with the intense movements within my upper body and longing for the process to end. The movements subside and finally return to normal. The shaman and I look at each other in bemusement. "Well, that was intense," I said.

We sit down and discuss what the hell has just happened. "You do realise you are working at such a high intensity and level, I wonder where all of this is going?" said the shaman. The shaman also mentions Snake spirit is still in my body, wrapped around my spine with two heads at the top supporting my jaw.

Snake will stay with me until the cleaning process is complete. I'm amused by this but also comforted by the protection of snake and don't doubt the honesty and truth of these words. I'm so pleased the shaman has witnessed all of this for I know the intensity of what I'm working with is off the spectrum but who could I share this with.

We discussed what each of us sensed, saw and felt. We were pretty much on the same page which was another first for me. I have friends that are mediums, but they don't experience the same intensity. I told the shaman I felt the device in the left side of my head being removed, but then it was put back on.

The shaman clarified she had removed it, in her words the metal plate, but had been told she was to put it back.

My guides throughout the session had been running the show and only allowed her to do what I needed. They had firmly insisted she put it immediately back. She also said I had the capability with my guides to remove the device.

I was made aware throughout the healing session I was capable of removing the device with my spirit guides. It was part of my development to remove it. The shaman said it would occur, but I needed to set time aside for my spirit team to work with me to remove it. I hadn't told the shaman that every day, I would lie in silence and let them work on me physically and spiritually.

I had also been told that this whole process would end exactly at the right time and it would be done by my team. I had been shown the finish line so many times, but questioned the realisation of the power of the spiritual world. I had just witnessed the power, dedication and love from the other side to get me back up and running.

More importantly, this gave me confirmation that all of what I had been experiencing was not all made up nonsense and simply in my head. Finally, someone else had witnessed my truth. Why now? We will have to wait and see. One thing is for sure, it must be something important for why would they invest so much time in me.

After that session, I felt more positive and accepted it would all work out but at the right time. When, how and where? I don't know. I felt honoured and humbled to be in the presence of a real shaman who could also see the spiritual world.

The shaman had a beautiful soul, with a pure heart, not only that but she understood the bigger picture of this journey. We are here for such a short time and the purpose is to firstly, be our true self and secondly, to spread as much healing, love and light whilst we are here.

As much as the material world and possessions are nice, it can't truly fulfil you and you certainly can't take material possessions with you. You only ever borrow things, nothing belongs to you, including people.

I admired the shaman for she was unapologetic of who she was, what she was and more importantly was working with the gifts she had been given.

I realised I still had a lot to learn and an inner knowing that my true purpose/ journey had only just begun.

LIFE CONTINUES

It takes me a few days to process what has happened. I try to describe to Tony what happened. He sits quietly and listens, then after a period of time says, "Bloody hell, Jane, that sounds like an awesome film." It always fascinates me the way my husband never judges the crazy things I share with him.

I can't imagine there are many husbands so accepting of what we discuss. I have friends that are mediums and they certainly don't tell their partners everything.

I sometimes wonder if perhaps one day he will turn around and say, "Right, Jane, that's enough, you have gone too far!" and insist I get professional help. I'm one hell of a lucky woman having such a supportive husband who takes everything in his stride.

Within a few weeks as the shaman said she would do, she put on a workshop to teach spiritual/energy protection. I now know I must switch on. I have heard from many people working spiritually that you don't need to protect yourself as everything is all about the intention you put out into the world.

I was taught by a very well respected medium that darkness can't come your way as you are surrounded by love, light and always protected. At the time, I strongly disagreed as surely the world is made up of light and dark.

I felt her naivety to be a little silly. I had shared my view with a fellow member in the group who got worried, a little scared and told the teacher what I had said. The following week in our circle, I got a severe dressing down that we were fully protected and it was all about our intention.

I felt really angry and furious inside, but smiled sweetly and apologised. This teacher was known as one of the best and to be quite honest, I wanted her wealth of knowledge. It took every ounce of control and strength to keep my mouth shut as I knew this to be wrong.

The medium who was frightened that day has developed beyond belief and is now very aware of dark and light energies. I have a theory that mediums become ill due to not protecting themselves properly. I thought I had been protecting myself, but obviously not very well.

As the shaman explained times have changed, frequency and energy are evolving and you need to keep up with it or get left behind. Well, I don't want to get left behind so now I need to learn as much as I can on protecting my energy.

You would think after all that healing I received, I would feel a bit better. I have this strange sensation inside my body, a whirling energy that is almost fighting to find a way to settle my spirit. It's best described as the depths of darkness and self-sabotage being infiltrated by a lighter, warmer, freer spirit tearing down the walls of past hurts and turmoil.

The past behaviour and thought processes are putting up a good fight to remain in power, but the strength and experience of the shaman's healing and my spirit team are too strong. I have no doubt this will settle down for I have been told the outcome.

The spiritual fight within causes the left side of my body to become enraged for whatever it is, it doesn't want to leave. I find myself lying in bed for prolonged periods of time as my balance regresses and the pain in my left eye is so severe it frightens me.

I feel nauseous with a stabbing pain that can only be described as a sharp knife repeatedly being plugged into my left eye. I find myself begging for someone to remove my eye. There is no option but to calmly observe the process unravel and I also know I cannot fuel the fear, for fear will only heighten the pain and strengthen the darkness within.

These episodes go on for four days before things start to return to my normal. My mum is the first to comment on my health and being religious questions me dabbling in shamanic healing.

I assure her it's all part of my journey and I need to go through this process to get over the finish line. "Jane, I wish you would stop messing around with your health and just leave it be," she told me. I reply, "If you think

I'm being stuck like this for the rest of my life, you can forget it. I'll take whatever risks I am led to take for I am completely in safe hands."

Mum replied, "Just saying you have got worse since doing that shaman healing." Secretly, my mum longs for me to go back to church, but she is not a deluded woman and knows that will never happen.

So, we have these wonderful conversations and I have to admire my Mum's ability to remain open. It was bad enough for me communicating with the spirit world, but now of all the things I could do, exploring shamanic healing really doesn't sit right with her.

She has read my channelled writings and come up with her own conclusion that we both believe in a divine energy which is pure and loving. My poor mum having a daughter like me but she loves me for who I am.

Please don't be put off if you feel drawn to see a shamanic healer for if you see a true healer they really are powerful healers and have the ability to remove energies that can hinder our time on earth. Always search for the best as it does concern me so many people attend short courses and set up practises.

I'm concerned not only for the patient but the healer for you could be taking on energies that could affect your health and mental well-being. A true healer, medium etc., are usually chosen whether they want to be or not.

There are so many ways we can help one another simply by giving one another time and speaking kind words. If you are born with true healing gifts, at some point in life you will need to use them to help others. Gifts are to be shared, but otherwise, please leave it alone.

SHAMANIC PROTECTION WORKSHOP

Not in my wildest dreams did I ever expect to attend a shamanic protection course. I also never expected to meet a true shaman healer upon my journey. I am open-minded, but I have never felt any desire to explore shamanism.

In the past, I had done a couple of shamanic journeying meditations, but never found it felt right for me and couldn't see how it would enhance my development. I have come to the realisation that it was because I hadn't met the right mentor.

What is it they say, the right teacher will appear when the student is ready to learn. I've witnessed what this shaman is capable of so I'm happy to be her student. A woman who is not only a powerful healer, but has the ability, wisdom and capability to remove darkness and infiltrate with loving light, pretty awesome!

The day of the shaman protection workshop arrives. I'm not sure how I feel because I'm not even sure this is right for me, yet my guides keep insisting this is the correct path. I'm glad when I'm greeted by the shaman for I don't know anyone else on the course. Her warm smile and loving energy immediately puts me at ease.

The group only consists of six people who I tune in quickly to see what characters we have. To my delight, all the ladies are gifted in different fields, some more in control than others over their gifts, but all good, kind and decent people.

There are several shamanic items I have never seen and certainly never worked with laid out in front of us. There are brass bowls with sage and Palo Santo which when burned removes negativity. There are drums, an unusual looking rattle, a beautiful large feather and a spray called shaman's spit.

I'm now fully engaged as firstly the environment feels safe, but how exciting I'm going to be taught new spiritual protection techniques that are thousands of years old. I suddenly felt honoured and privileged to have access to wisdom and healing techniques from the past. I'm really not sure what I am allowed to share with you, the reader, without offending the traditions of Shamanism.

Without going into too much detail, I was shown an old healing tradition that removes negative energy from often jealous people who do not wish us well on our journey. I was sceptical and over analytical with this tradition, but after seeing the results with my own eyes, I came to the conclusion there might be something in this. For now, I decide to sit on the fence until I'm taught more.

The workshop continued with techniques on how to protect ourselves which was fascinating, but I was blown away by a ritual where we visualised energy coming through our body whilst repeating powerful words from past scriptures.

The intensity and the privilege to experience such love, power and light from the spirit world was not only uplifting, but emotional. As we were doing this protection technique, I could see and feel my guides drawing closer and feel the love and excitement from the other side for it was so heightened. I was given reassurance and confirmation that this was exactly where and what I should be doing.

The strange thing was as the shaman would describe what we would do, my brain would immediately go into self-doubting mode, but then I would just do everything with ease as though I had done all of this before. I had a lot to digest, but I was disciplined and detached myself from my own thoughts. I decided I would reflect and analyse all of this later.

As a medium, you become disciplined at stilling the mind and not allowing the material world to come in until the time is right. I have been given permission from my guides to tell you about the final part of the workshop as this is my experience and nobody else's.

In Shamanism, they believe we all have different power spirit animals that help us in different capacities, for example protection, energy, knowledge, peace, fun, etc. Once we are taught how to access the different worlds, we can call upon these spirit animals to help us and perhaps in time through healing, help others. I've heard this before, but not really given it much thought. I like listening to others' views but it only resonates with me when I get to experience things for myself, then I decide what my truth is.

The teacher informs us we are going to do a meditation, a journey to meet our spirit protection power animal.

We can choose our animal or wait and see what we are given. I'm definitely going to see what I am given for I know the spirit world is so superior to us in intelligence and everything.

As the teacher talks before she says the words, I can already see a deep blue door, slightly open down a brilliant white corridor. I tell myself off and remind myself to stay focused on what the teacher is telling us.

She tells us there is a door in front of us. As she continues to speak, we become closer to the door which is open. We step through the door into a beautiful, flourishing green forest. Everything in the forest feels alive with growth, vitality and a surreal energy.

The air smells crisp and fresh with a subtle hint of fresh wet grass and fragrances again I can't articulate for there is nothing to compare them to on this earth.

My eyes are drawn to the different vibrant shades of

green, flowers, that I don't recognise in full bloom and I can hear the sound of insects.

I'm trying to take in as much as I can before we are told to carry on walking through the forest along a path. At the end of the path, we will meet our protection spirit animal guide. As I'm walking along the path, I clearly see a wolf's face close to mine. I decide to walk a little further and once again the wolf appears. The wolf is crystal clear and once again very close to my face.

The wolf is white but has a few flicks of grey by its ears and on top of its head but not many. The eyes are a beautiful, rusty deep orange which I can't seem to take my eyes off. The eyes have so many depths to them consisting of truth, wisdom and almost tribal knowledge. I then hear the teacher say spend some time with your animal guide and blend with them. I feel so strongly drawn to the wolf's eyes as though they are drawing me in.

As I look deeper into the wolf's eyes, I notice they have changed into the exact same colour and distinct markings of my eyes. I am looking directly into my own eyes but they are inside the wolf. How can this be?

We have become one. I have become the wolf and the wolf has become me; we are within one another's bodies. I feel strong, powerful and primal. I'm a little horrified that I am going to admit to this, but here goes, I feel like a wild wolf who will protect and kill if necessary to the death if anyone tries to harm me. I notice these sensations are a little extreme, a little frightening and immediately remove myself from the wolf's body.

The wolf stood to the right side of me as I stroked its soft white fur. We, through that experience, have become one. I have no doubts that in the future, I am one hundred percent protected by this beautiful, powerful and very protective animal. My guides know how I work, I need to see, sense and feel things for myself to be convinced. I'm convinced!

Something inside of me has changed, I feel strong, safe, protected and emotional for I wasn't expecting any of that. As I'm happily spending time bonding with this amazing, beautiful and mystical creature, I'm shown a vision of the wolf behaving like an over excited dog bringing me a snake in his mouth.

The snake isn't moving and appears to be quite happy and calm being held between the jaws of this wolf. I hear the teacher telling us to start coming back out of the meditation.

I lie there feeling a little speechless for I had no idea how powerful this meditation was going to be for I've never experienced anything so magical before. We all go around the room and discuss one by one what animal we got. Finally, it gets to me and I say I got a wolf.

The teacher says that's one animal you can't pick for the wolf has to pick you. Also, Jane, where you see one wolf there are always many so you have a pack of wolves protecting you. I then told her how our bodies had blended and how I felt powerful and a little wild.

She looked a little bit unsure what I had just admitted to but seemed happy when I revealed, I had stepped out of the wolf's body and taken control of the intensity of the situation.

I just needed more time to get used to the wolf, I think I had taken it a bit fast. I then admitted to the vision where I had seen the wolf carrying a snake in its mouth (Too much information, perhaps!). I just wanted to understand and learn everything.

The teacher then explained the importance of the spirit snake which is predominately for healing. In the previous healings I had had with the shaman, we had already witnessed the snake and both seen wolves around me.

So clever all this Shaman healing stuff! When I got home, I literally couldn't stop thinking about the workshop, it felt once again so comfortable and familiar. The excitement of my guides and the power and protection of that beautiful wolf simply blew me away. I felt confused, the last seventeen years I had spent perfecting my mediumship and psychic skills.

I felt truly alive and at my best when I channelled

writings, but nothing felt as right or powerful as this. It felt so right I questioned what the hell my spirit guides had in mind for me. The logical side of my brain was saying, "Jane, just stick to what you have been doing, you're good at it, don't complicate things but I also have to admit that throughout this life I've always had this inner feeling that I haven't fulfilled my full potential.

I know I have a lot more to give, but just hadn't so far found the right keys to unlock the right doors. I decided I needed time to step back and have time to see where all of this was going. I knew the answer but really didn't want to get this one wrong.

NO SHOCK, BUT A SURPRISE

I'm usually very accepting of spiritual experiences but the problem with the Shaman healing and workshop was it unsettled me firstly how at ease I was with it all and secondly, how I had a deep knowing I had done all of this before.

When I have questions, I need answers to, I sit down at my computer and channel.

I was reluctant to ask, for I almost didn't want the truth which interested me why I felt this way. I knew there was a six week in depth Shaman course which consisted of daily practises, so it was a huge commitment.

I couldn't stop thinking about the course, how was I even going to approach Tony to tell him that every weekend for six weeks, I would be attending lessons on Shamanism.

No first, I needed to check I wasn't getting over excited and going down the wrong path. Finally, I made myself sit down and ask my guides should I really be going down the Shaman route? This is what I received.

Shaman Course?

Is the shaman teacher all that she seems

I feel like I've lost the ability to see

Wait

Look around

Why can't you see the reality?

The reality my dear

Is how you sense, feel and think

We have spent much time working with you

You sensed a belonging

Is this not true

You felt safe, alive and new

Was this also not true

So what is your truth?

One of cards and a mystical path

Or a road of truth

Stoved upon you

Yes, my dear

Go ahead

Walk the path in front of you

This is a new beginning

One of healing and truth

This course is exactly designed for you

You might question this path

But what has happened so far

A path of control

Control doesn't exist

Just manufactured by you, to kid yourself you are true

The reality my dear is

This path was meant for you

It will bring enlightenment, healing and truth

No more playing at a lower level

Time to rise to the new heights

The heights that brought you here in this time

You will see what we mean

This is not for you to over analyse

Just keep stepping forward

For the path awaits

And as you have seen there is nothing to hinder your path

All we ask

Is for you to walk this path

A path of freedom

A path of truth

Most important a path to help those who also see, sense, and feel like you.

So, the decision had been made, it felt right, although my logical mind still felt a little amused by the prospect of exploring Shamanism. One thing I have learnt throughout my life is my spiritual guides know exactly what I should be doing and what I shouldn't be doing.

I don't always listen and have learnt the hard way several times, but I think it is healthy to question. I can't bear the prospect of turning completely into a free spirit for that would be giving up all control.

I have come to the realisation that this journey definitely runs smoother when I listen. I'm getting better and who knows, hopefully, in this lifetime I will finally completely trust.

The other thing that has changed since having Shamanic healing sessions and bathing in the energy is my dreams have become calmer. I still dream, but not so intensely which I'm rather enjoying. I can't work out whether this is a good thing, but I'm certainly enjoying waking up and feeling like I had slept. I feel calmer, wiser and now more vulnerable.

The last one I'm not so keen on, but it feels like I've grown up, strange choice of words! But that's how I feel. I feel ready to take responsibility for my health and well-being.

The other day I was having a chat with a very good friend and she asked me to tune in and answer a question for her and I said quite firmly, "No!" I was shocked by my reply and explained I'm not using my energy unless I need to. "You know it makes me feel sick, so no! It's time I started listening, I need to start listening.

Unless they want me to use my skills, then I'm not doing it," I said. Yikes! That was rather firm and a little rude. I immediately apologised, but felt a mixture of guilt and empowerment. Finally, the penny has dropped, I will not use my energy unless I'm given permission and secondly, I need my energy to recover. Such a shame it has taken so bloody long! Oh well, we eventually got there in the end.

The other thing I have noticed after my Shaman

encounters is although I'm feeling calmer, I'm starting to have flashbacks and memories from my childhood. Memories will pop into my head whilst I'm washing up that I haven't thought about in years and I'd literally forgotten about.

I suddenly remember when I was seven years old and had just moved up from infants to the junior school. This was a huge transition in my life because I was going into big school and found the whole experience extremely frightening. I was a very polite, quiet, and conforming child who feared authority and would do everything not to bring attention to myself. The only thing I enjoyed about school was play time where I could run around outside in the fresh air playing football with the boys. Anyway, this one lunch time, it was pouring with rain so we had to stay indoors. I remember it was chaos, we were unsupervised and everyone was behaving like caged animals shouting and laughing.

One of the boys had got his hands on a football and it was being kicked around the room. The ball comes over to me and my first reaction is to kick it back. Time all of a sudden slows down as this ball flies in the air in slow motion, my heart sinks as I pray with all my might for the ball to stop. The ball hits the crucifix of the wall, it falls to the ground and smashes.

The whole class gasped! The room is silent, every single child looks at me horrified. "Please, don't tell the teacher. I'll give you anything, my lunch, my chocolate penguin, anything!" I begged.

The teacher walks in, the room is silent and the crucifix is laid broken in pieces on the floor. The male teacher shouts, "Who did this? The colour drains from my face, I'm frozen, unable to move due to fear and my heart is pumping out of my chest.

I'm begging God to help me get out of this mess. Immediately one of the children points his finger towards me and says, "Jane did it, sir!"

As I stood there, the teacher moved closer and started to shout in my face saying, "You are a wicked girl, God's crucifix. He died on the cross for us and you repay him with this." I was so frightened, horrified, embarrassed and ashamed I couldn't talk.

I remember vividly the anger and hatred in these large male adult eyes as his intimidating presence invades my space. "What have you got to say for yourself, speak child, speak!" he shouted in my face. I shakily replied, "I'm so sorry, I really didn't mean it, it was an accident." The class was deadly quiet as this enraged grown man lost control of himself still shouting at what an awful sin I had committed.

Eventually, to my relief, he sent me out of the class.

When I was finally allowed back into the classroom, the teacher had composed himself. He calmly explained to the class how awful and wicked I was and then gave me my sentence in front of what felt like a jury. The punishment for the crime was to stay in every lunch break and write neatly with no spelling mistakes one hundred lines. "I must not play football during wet weather breaks!" (I still remember that sentence).

Every lunch break, I was sent to a small room, it had a desk and chair with nothing on the walls. To a seven-year-old's imagination, I suppose it's a little like a prison.

The staff room was further up the corridor and the teachers would ignore me or look disapproving down their noses at the wicked child. The whole school, much to my embarrassment, had been informed what had happened and all the children were forbidden to look or talk to me.

If any child was caught smiling or talking to me, they would also be punished. Whilst writing, I must not play football during wet weather breaks, my tiny hand used to cramp up.

I would anxiously keep checking if my writing was neat enough and I hadn't made any spelling mistakes. Daily, the teacher would remind me that if I made any mistakes I would have to start from the beginning. (Oh, the good old days, they really catered for children's mental well-being, such fun!) I felt a mixture of emotions from humiliation, sadness, shame, but this continual pit of anxiety running through my veins.

I was secretly a very anxious child so literally the only pleasure in attending that rigid catholic school was lunch break. I needed the fresh air, the freedom to express myself through playing football for what those teachers never knew was that football was my saviour.

Looking back through adult eyes, I can recognise now why perhaps I had locked that experience away. It seems rather trivial, but to Jane, the seven-year-old child, all the feelings must have been horrendous.

Finally, I was let free out of the prison and assured the subject would not be mentioned again. I have to compliment my teacher for he never mentioned it again, but I was also very much aware he had frightened himself with his lack of control and raging anger over the situation and felt a little remorseful. (The good old days, when school was a laugh a minute!)

The flashbacks of my childhood continue. It's as though I had to revisit them to process the emotions which in time will perhaps be released. I also experience memories I have buried so deep I had forgotten them.

Fascinating, as adults, we think we have processed and forgiven past events but we forget about the child's feelings at the time and as ourselves we naturally push forwards and don't allow the child part of us to also process and forgive. I've never thought of this in that way, yet it makes perfect sense. I know as Jane today,

I'm happy with my past.

I'm being taught by this latest experience you can't fully heal unless you allow yourself to hear, feel, sense and shout what the inner child is saying. I have one memory as a child that as an adult still upsets me. I often wonder why this past experience has still got the power to haunt me. I have processed it and spoken openly with a trusted friend but still it lurks around.

The penny has dropped. Instead of looking at it with my adult eyes, I have to process it with my child's eyes. I have never given Jane the child permission to release her feelings of anxiety, fear, sadness and perhaps even anger to forgive the past.

I really don't understand the full power of Shamanic healing, but I do know it has given me clarity, compassion and wisdom.

Something very powerful has occurred within me, I also know layers upon layers of perhaps past lives, turmoil, hidden secrets and emotions are being let free. It's a strange concept and I'm cringing as I type this as I have very little knowledge on any of this, but I also know these words to be true.

As the childhood memories draw to an end for the time being, I feel so different. Something significant has spiritually changed within me. I feel like I'm moving forwards and in the right direction. I feel as both a child and an adult I have been searching for this feeling within that I'm finally on the right path.

I feel like I'm at exactly the right place at the right time doing and being what I should be, me! Gosh, I hope this feeling lasts for I like it!

SHAMANIC WAY - A SIX WEEK COURSE

I've had too much time to analyse whether I should be doing a Shamanic course. Really, a shamanic course!

Too late, I've signed up for it now. I don't know what to expect, feeling sceptical but I'm open-minded. I keep questioning my spirit guides to check they have got this one right, but they insist I need to do it. I agree to do it but they also know I need proof to be convinced.

Now I'm not about to reveal the exact procedures we were taught and if I did I'm sure firstly I would explain it wrong and secondly it would upset and be disrespectful to the shaman community. What I am prepared to share with you is my experience.

I have met so many people who recite spiritual books they have read, but I always discipline myself not to read others' interpretation of what to expect on a spiritual journey.

I know very little about Shamanism and want to witness, feel, sense and absorb it all how the spirit world want me to receive it. I have been assured I am one hundred percent protected which is good enough for me.

I do know one thing and that is most other mediums won't go near it perhaps due to fear as it doesn't get the same gentle press as an uplifting Reiki course.

When I told my friend Clarissa about the course, she seemed a little unsure and sceptical which made me laugh as I reminded her that mediums happily speak to so-called dead people, but exploring one of the oldest tribal healing methods with our spirit world is unconceivable.

I shall have to find out for myself what is so scary about the shamanic world.

Yikes! I hope I have got this one right. I've just realised how much I have changed.

Six or seven years ago, I would never have entertained anything other than mediumship and perhaps a bit of Reiki, but now I have a thirst for knowledge and development. Why? Because I have this inner knowing we have limited time on earth and I'm not here to play at all this spiritual stuff.

To perfect the gifts we have will not only protect our health, but really help others. The things I have experienced have opened my mind to the fact that there are higher energies that not only can make people feel better, but help them heal.

I Know I am protected by my spirit team, they are the ones who have led and given permission to explore different methods.

Surely it would be morally wrong for me not to develop due to self-inflicted fear?

Don't get me wrong, I'm not going to start volunteering to mess around with energy that feels wrong, but I have an obligation to listen, trust and follow my path. Goodness, did I just say that?

First day of the course, there were four of us. A bunch of lovely ladies, we are all from different backgrounds and to my delight, all relatable.

The shaman explains the background to how Shamanism became widely used in the Western world.

A very well-known anthropologist (anthropologists study the origin, development and behaviour of humans) studied the behaviour of shamans. The tribal community he observed would take the drug ayahuasca which would make people dance around with no inhibitions before collapsing on the floor.

Whilst the people were basically out of it, they would experience information from the spirit world and come back with insight and information that they couldn't have known. The drug, if taken by westerners, was so dangerous it could and did kill people.

This anthropologist worked out scientifically that a continuous rhythm of drumming/rattling/didgeridooing provides the same level of theta brain waves enabling us without taking the drug to journey and receive spiritual insight from other worlds.

To be effective, the drumming needs to be 4 plus beats a second. What a clever bloke! Much to my relief, we wouldn't be taking any ayahuasca today.

Please do not quote what I have just explained to you in very simple words as I have explained this journey in my words, not necessarily explained in exactly the right words. (Google it, perhaps.)

I'm impressed with what I have been taught as at least there has been some study behind what we are about to explore. The teacher is also knowledgeable, kind, patient and you immediately know you are in safe hands.

I have already seen her healing capabilities and have no doubt we are learning from one of the best. To anyone thinking about exploring shamanism, please do your homework for as in all walks of life there are good and bad.

This is one spiritual practise that you can't afford to get wrong.

The teacher continues to explain we will be visiting through a drumming technique transcended, enlightened, compassionate, loving, wise and all-knowing spirits. We will be visiting parallel universes which are outside of time and space.

There are, in shamanism, three levels: the lower world, upper world and middle world.

We will be visiting the lower world and the upper world. Yikes! Wait a minute, did she just mention the lower world? I'm a little unnerved because in the catholic faith isn't that where Satan and the baddies hang out?

Time to ask more questions, I can feel my past childhood deep fears rear their ugly heads. I express my concerns to the teacher who immediately explains what the lower world is.

The lower world is in my simplicity everything to do with the animal kingdom, nature, mother earth, grounding, not what we are led to believe. We are taught the right place to go to, the correct intention and words to say which with the drumming will give us access to the lower world.

Today, we will be meeting our power animal spirit which will provide us with protection. I won't lie, I'm feeling a little concerned for I am literally going into the unknown.

As I think this, my guides draw closer reassuring me I am totally safe and protected. My poor mum is going to be horrified when she reads this, but then I suppose so will everyone that knows me!

The drumming begins, within a few minutes, all the worries have vanished and I find myself falling down dark tunnels journeying further and further into the depths of earth. Some of the tunnels are swirly and others it feels like you are falling in nothing but air.

Finally, much to my relief, I land gently and with precision on my feet. I notice my feet are bare and the ground feels fresh and crisp upon my toes. I look around and I'm welcomed by a tribal community that seem to know me and are excited I have arrived.

I feel strangely at home, emotional and happy. I start to look around for my power animal. I notice a wolf come to greet me but just as I think this is my power animal, the wolf and the tribe step to the side showing me what I need to connect to. I see the most beautiful and enormous elephant looking straight into my eyes.

The intensity of the stare is mesmerising. I'm drawn into the gentle brown eyes and I notice how long the elephant's eyelashes are. The eye gives me such depth of wisdom and knowledge. I'm told I will be able to see further than most.

I am protected and part of the herd. As this is spoken, I see hundreds of elephants gather in a circle formation around me. I feel part of the herd and overcome with the sense of protection. I notice a singular tree in the distance, before a baby elephant is introduced to me that makes me smile and fills my heart with comfort and joy. The baby elephant I am told symbolises new beginnings, new opportunities and excitement.

How do I know this? Because the information is being downloaded in a different method, maybe telepathic, not the same as channelling, but very similar. The circle formation of the herd disperses. We all mix as though getting to know each other's energy.

I feel welcomed and part of the herd, strong, protected and safe. I feel so content and blissfully happy. A world where everything is pure, simple without any hidden agenda. I hear the sound of the drumming changing to the beat which means it's time to return back.

I feel to my bemusement a sense of sadness for I've never felt acceptance and contentment in the real world to this degree. We all return from our journeying, all having different experiences but all uplifting, positive and profound.

What has just happened? I need time to process this but after we have discussed our journeys, the teacher is keen to take us to the upper world to experience the difference.

Once again, we go through a set procedure, but this time our intention is to journey to the upper world. I feel no apprehension, just intrigued to find out whether there is any substance to this spiritual process. Before I know it, I am soaring higher and higher into the sky. I feel so free, happy, content and a knowing that this is a privilege to feel this sensation.

I find myself questioning the reality of what I am

experiencing and quickly remind myself to discipline my thinking mind and go with the process. I will not question until the end. As ridiculous as it might sound, I am flying above the clouds and it's blissful.

Suddenly out of nowhere, my feet land on the ground. I'm barefooted and stood on top of an enormous mountain which I know I have visited several times before.

I immediately know I have been here before as a child. The memories and connections come flooding back. This was my safe place as a child in a previous life. I have sat here before with a tribal grandfather who has previously taught me past knowledge.

We used to sit on the mountain watching eagles fly and dance in the sky. I suddenly feel like that innocent, pure child on the beginning of her journey about to absorb the wealth of knowledge from the wise, tribal grandfather figure. I quickly remind myself why I am here. I am here to connect with a teacher.

I'm looking around to see if I can find a spiritual teacher. I feel a male presence who appears in an angelic form. Angelic form as you would imagine in some sort of white robe, but strangely, I choose not to accept this appearance, but I accept the presence.

Why? I suppose to let the spiritual world I am accepting of the true essence not the display humans are given to comfort them. I like to see, but sensing, feeling and knowing a pure source is more powerful. I'm given a heart-shaped pink rose quartz which is placed into my left hand.

The rose quartz is for me to heal and then to go on to heal others. I feel humbled by the physical touch upon my left hand. I ask what is it they want me to do, what is my gift?

The presence draws closer and whispers in my ear, "Healing." Bloody hell, I actually heard it, not in my thoughts but in my ear. Yikes! I'm then shown past images as though I'm watching a film of past tribal healers.

I'm shown some sort of tribal wooden stick with feathers and strange white chalky rocks or bones on it. As I'm taking in as much knowledge as I can, I start to receive healing. My body radiates this blissful warmth. My head is stretched over to the right and my eyes are rolling uncontrollably up and backwards.

We are all wearing black out eye masks so I'm comfortable to let the process take its course as I know the others in the group will not know or witness what is occurring. The sound of the drum beat changes informing us it is time to return to the real world.

The teacher comments as she had previously witnessed the extreme healing I receive that I wasn't being physically moved as much as before.

I told her that in a group session I would not allow others to see this so I wouldn't allow myself to fully go into a trance state.

Thank goodness, we all had eye masks on otherwise, I think I would have literally scared the hell out of everyone. It's only the first session so I'm not about to declare my truth to a bunch of strangers, however open-minded and liberal they are.

Wow what has just happened? I need time to process all this crazy, mind-blowing stuff and put it into some sort of logical Jane box.

Before we leave, we are given daily homework to do. We will be journeying by ourselves to the lower and upper worlds to connect to our power animals and spiritual guides.

We will document what we experience and discuss and review what we have found for the next weekend. I won't lie, I leave that course unable to speak because I have no words to describe what I have witnessed and how I am feeling.

I decide I need a day off to process and connect with the material world before dedicating myself to journeying on the following Monday. I'm already aware I am safe and protected. If Spirit want me to do this, then I'm not playing at it. I shall commit one hundred percent.

REALITY OR SIMPLY IMAGINATION?

I'm in the privacy and safety of my home so I'm eager to find out what's real. I can fully submerge myself into the process and I have no intentions of holding anything back. The spirit world wants me to do this so I will discover why. I commit myself to daily journeying to the upper world and the lower world.

The process and journeying is becoming second nature and the messages I'm receiving are beautiful, but it will take more to fully convince me. I continue to journey religiously every day, some days twice. The lower world is comforting to spend time in.

What do I mean by this? It feels familiar, more earthy, grounding, safe and natural. It's like you are encased in a sense of pure love, acceptance and given special time out to breath, even cry, it's basically blissful.

Dare I say it, it's not as challenging as the upper world which forces you to face your truth, your reality and face perhaps your hidden fears. The upper world is no messing, you will learn, heal and move forwards on your chosen journey. You will also in time be shown how the spirit world wants to utilise your gifts on earth.

Others will disagree with what I have just said, but as I have said all along, this is only from my experience. Every individual has and will experience their journey differently and if you are genuinely chosen to work with the spirit world to help heal others, you will be given exactly what is right for you.

I have noticed the sound of the drumming is making me feel more relaxed, calmer and my sleep has improved, which is a bonus. I wake up in the morning and feel rested which I'm sad to say I can't remember the last time I had this sensation.

I feel like I've slept! I'm definitely witnessing an inner change and have already identified there is without any doubt something very real and strong in this shaman technique. I'm eager to learn more.

I've also noticed the apprehension or fear I initially had towards shamanism has gone for I have a knowing I have complete control. Where and how did that happen? The honest answer, I don't know! I feel layers of my old self being removed and a more content, accepting and chilled out Jane developing. I like it!

The course is intense and the spiritual development is fast. By this I mean you are learning and absorbing new techniques and knowledge rapidly. You need a week in between to process all the humbling and mind-boggling experiences. I do think it helps having worked with some of the most disciplined old school mediums.

These selfless mediums have installed discipline, knowledge and tools to discipline the mind and work as a pure channel. I wouldn't recommend learning shamanism unless you have a calling and a desire to do something positive with it as even I have found it at times to stretch the boundaries of the mind.

Someone less experienced could venture into territory that could potentially frighten them. Although saying that if you find the right teacher, you should be in safe hands. I have been fortunate to always stumble across the best teachers, but I have spoken to people who haven't had good experiences, but this is more related to mediumship teachers.

If a teacher is full of themselves and keeps telling you how amazing they are, this is due to their own ego. To be an effective teacher, surely the ego must be removed to benefit and put the best interests of the students first.

A good spiritual teacher will show humbleness and a desire to produce humble, gifted students, who have the desire to put love back into this world.

There is good and bad in every walk of life so my tip would be to listen to your own instincts and don't question yourself. Sometimes in life you may feel something or someone isn't what they appear. Most of us tell ourselves we are being silly and overreacting. In time, you inevitably find out further down the line, you were right all along and kicking yourself for not listening to your instincts.

Just because someone tells you they are an expert

doesn't mean they are and certainly doesn't mean they are any good. LISTEN TO YOUR INSTINCTS!

The course continues and we are taught how to connect to our true essence and then how to connect others to their true essence.

I won't lie, whilst doing the process, it was perfectly normal and real, but once I gave myself time to analyse the process, it blew my mind.

So, what do I mean by connecting to your true essence? Basically, you journey to the lower world or the higher world whichever you are drawn or told to go to. Once you are in your chosen world, you ask to see your or someone else's true essence.

The true essence is what the person was before they came down to earth and became what either they were told to be or thought they should be rather than being their true self. Fascinating and a little sad that so many of us are not being our true selves and fulfilling our true purpose.

I am totally guilty of wanting to fit into society and have been scared of ridicule and what others think. It takes a brave person to follow their true path and not give a hoot what others think.

I'm too tired pretending to be a middle-class, mother, friend, wife and considered by society to be normal. I don't know what normal means but I'm tired of trying to be it, so I've decided I'm no longer going to. Now before journeying to the upper world, I questioned the whole process and suspected this could have been a load of rubbish, but I was proven wrong. Let me share my experience with you.

I will not reveal the Shaman techniques as this would be disrespectful, possibly dangerous, but more importantly should only be taught by an experienced teacher. I can tell you, we all go to a specific place in our minds before sending out a clear and precise intention on which world we will visit and what we wish to discover. I'm sceptical as I'm not convinced you can meet and reconnect to your true essence.

I discipline my mind and allow myself to enter a trance state whilst listening to the drumming. Within seconds, I'm in the upper world having a look around. I can genuinely say all of this feels so comforting and familiar. I see a transparent cord attached to me which I know is attached to something.

As I take another look, I meet a young, handsome, fresh-faced black boy. He looks about 17 years old, barefoot, and wearing some sort of tribal skirt. I notice he has a band around his upper arm which has some sort of feathers around it. He is also wearing a necklace with lots of small white sharp teeth on it which I presume for some reason are crocodile teeth?

I wasn't expecting that. It fascinates me this journeying

as I haven't got the imagination to conjure up what I'm led to witness. We are communicating I presume by thought and it feels completely normal. His energy is full of vitality, excitement and a thirst for exploring and discovering new methods, especially scientific information related to the body.

He shows me him exploring nature, discovering new herbs and he has a love and respect for nature. Everything in nature is to be respected as it is such a fine balance in the ecological chain.

He is a natural leader without dictating and he enjoys passing on his knowledge to those who want to learn. People are naturally drawn to him and want to learn from him.

He is a life lover! Being in his presence feels me with hope, energy and an overwhelming excitement and thirst for living. "There is so much more to discover, but it is so important to share the knowledge with those who are ready to receive it" he tells me.

I ask him what my true purpose is, he looks at me amused as though I should already know this. "You are fit, strong, powerful and healthy.

You are a healer, you are to heal people and animals. You will pass on what you discover to help others," he replied looking amused.

The drumming begins to change, signalling it is time to

journey back. I say goodbye and return to the here and now. I sat in the group questioning whether I could have imagined all of that, yet, it was so real. And why would I choose to imagine a young tribal boy when surely through choice I could have imagined an angel?

At the end of each session, I struggle to talk or articulate what I have witnessed for there aren't any words. I tend to find myself speechless and need time to work out how, what, why has all of this happened. I know it is all real, but find myself repeatedly questioning myself.

As I have said before, I need proof and I'm not easily convinced. The whole journeying is so real, dare I say, more real than this world. It takes a good week for me to sit back on the fence, remaining open-minded to the whole process.

I do question the words he used that I am fit, strong and healthy. Maybe it's me that has created my ill health by listening to the diagnosis I have been given by doctors? I have never chosen to embrace or accept the doctor's diagnosis for I'm a believer that once you are told and accept a medical diagnosis then it can become you and you become it (This opinion is for me and is definitely not related to any other!).

Well obviously, I didn't do a good enough job because my inner true self knows I am a strong, healthy and a life-loving person. I take comfort that I am reconnected to my true self and I'm back on track to living a full, exciting and fulfilling life.

I completely resonated with my true essence and identified immediately that was what I wanted most out of this life but had simply lost my way.

The interesting thing was we were given the tools and techniques to reconnect others to their true essence. The person each time on the end of the translucent cord was always a complete surprise and never what you could have imagined.

The fascinating part was each person you reconnected with their true self could completely identify with the essence of themselves. I did this on my husband and found out so much more about him and what truly fulfilled him and what he should and really wanted to do in this lifetime.

Life, paying bills, society and believing in what we think we should do often to appease parents or beliefs we are born into can take us down the wrong route.

I also observed myself and others felt more calm, self-accepting and happier as though they were fully connected – almost whole. I don't profess to understand fully how all of this works, but it seems to bring positivity, contentment and love back into a person's life so surely that's a good thing?

None of this makes logical sense, but it has profound effects. I shall continue to sit on the fence, but with each experience I'm becoming more and more convinced. I'm just still fighting with the logical side of my brain.

TIME TO CONNECT TO OUR HEALING PARTNERS

The daily practice of journeying to the upper world and lower worlds is becoming second nature. It's fascinating how adaptable the mind and body is once you remove fear and self- intimidation out of the way. Fear really is created by our own thoughts, if you break it down to basics, we are completely in control.

The mind is so delicate, fill it with fear and repetitive thoughts spiralling out of control and you create your own personalised prison. Remove or control fear, the prison doors open allowing you access to contentment, happiness and freedom. I wish I had worked this one out years ago as fear is rather exhausting and all consuming.

Today, we are given the choice to journey to either visit the upper or the lower world to meet our healing guides. Once you connect to your healing guides you can call upon them or if you choose, work with them perhaps to help others heal in the future.

The drumming begins, we all put out our intentions and within seconds, I'm looking around in the upper world.

The drumming is a great tool for it keeps your mind relaxed and stops the mind wandering off by itself.

I'm greeted by an Indian healer, originally his feathers

on his head-dress were white and then turned to brown eagle feathers.

I'm staring straight into his intense, strong, but gentle warm, brown eyes. I know him as I recognise him as the man I have sat with on top of a mountain watching the eagles dance in the sky as a child. He shows me a blanket which I have seen before draped over both of us. His strong fatherly arms are protecting me from the chill and the often harsh elements of nature.

He feels protective, wise, gentle, loving, but more importantly, I know him! He strokes my hands which I can physically feel and puts a rose quartz in each palm. My hands feel like they are being activated, what do I mean by this?

My hands are really warm and I can feel this prickly sensation in my palms which feels again familiar and right. The rose quartz symbolises love. My hands will only be used for love and healing. I then hear him say, "You are a healer, you are one of us." As he says this I see and feel lots of beings surrounding us which is overwhelming with pure love. He continues to say, "Jane, you are part of our team. You must write, write with all your might, little one. You are to be a voice, your voice must get out. You will heal man and animals alike, 'healer.'

Suddenly I was in a swirling funnel of air. I can feel the air swirling around my body as though cleansing me.

I'm then rolling again and again as though I'm doing forward roll after forward roll as though I'm in some sort of spiritual energy tumble dryer. I see a wooden spear put through the centre of my body and now I'm being spun faster and faster like a helicopter blade.

I ask why is this happening? I'm told to deactivate devices in my body! (Really!) The devices are preventing me from using my true gifts.

Eventually the spinning stops and I'm showered in golden light which is mesmerising and comforting. The sound of the drumming is vibrating against the left side of my head and it feels like something is being released, it feels looser and as though something inside my head is trying to be removed.

Why? I'm shown some sort of robotic device inside my head which is wrapped around the left side of my jaw almost like a headpiece working on the telephones.

I'm then shown a strange metal looking device in my left eye which when uncovered has a piercing red laser.

The device has been deactivated and feels calm but I can see it hasn't been removed. The drumming beat changes, it's time to journey back.

I have no words to justify how I'm feeling. I feel upset, horrified, disturbed and questioning my sanity. Why, what is it and how?

We go around the group discussing our experiences whilst journeying and everyone has uplifting, healing, positive and pleasant experiences. I won't lie, I'm debating whether to tell the whole truth and maybe just mention the more pleasant bits. It's my turn, I decide to hold nothing back and tell the whole truth in the hope I was simply getting carried away with my imagination.

I can see the amusement in some of the members, but when I look at my teacher, she confirms it all made perfect sense for me and I was correct in what I had witnessed. Yikes! Can my world get any more crazy, can I not do anything normally? I need time to process and speak to my guides. Surely, they will disagree? They also agreed!

I resort to the old Jane and start over analysing what I have seen. I feel a mixture of bemusement, wrapped in a strange nothingness and I feel a little tainted. What do I mean by this? Well, let's be honest, I would have preferred to have seen myself as some sort of angelic angel not a weird half human, robotic, creepy creature.

I need to understand more, my mind is racing away with the situation. I decided to write a list of questions for my guides. I know I will only be given the truth, also I know they will only answer the questions I can process at this specific time.

I'm told rather harshly that I am no good to anyone if I

can't hold it together and that I'm useless without the sanity of my mind. Not the words I had hoped for, yet it quickly pulled me together. I'm working with energy that is to be respected and I have discovered the shamanic techniques are simply a stepping stone and giving me access to the energy I need to be working in.

I'm not stupid, shamanic healing doesn't work with robotic devices unless there is something I haven't been taught. I decide to pull myself together and put what I see into perspective or I have to walk away. The option of mental ill-health is not an option when I have full control.

Those frank words had a profound effect on me. It's time to start believing in myself!

THE HEALING BEGINS

I'm excited today as we are being taught the basic shamanic techniques to perform healing on one another within our group. I don't know what to expect, but I have the ability to discipline my mind to remain open and go with the flow. The drumming starts, we send out our intentions and choose which world we will journey to.

I'm immediately drawn to work in the higher world for this person. I blend with my healer and within seconds, I'm drawn into her body looking at her heart. I can see a shadow behind her heart which I automatically know needs removing but needs to be gently removed with precision. Might sound a little creepy but my guide shows me his hand placed over the top of mine and we become one.

He tells me the heart is full of past hurt emotions that were so painful it has created a dark shadow. Our hands naturally reach inside the body to remove the shadow but as we look at it there is a cord attached to the shadow.

We very gently, with our hand twist the cord, pull and detach it. As our hands are removed, he makes me look at it before it is removed from our hands into an invisible funnel of swirling air like a vacuum device which is taken to another dimension (I appreciate this sounds deluded but this is what happened!).

We go back to the heart area and start using a grey clay substance to seal the area. Blue fluid is then placed gently over the heart area as though calming down emotions and promoting healing followed by us finally pushing gold light into the heart.

He makes me check to see if we have completed the healing properly as if I'm his apprentice. "I'm happy we have done a good job," he nods. My eyes are then immediately drawn to the lady's ovaries, especially the right, but I can see both need healing. I'm looking inside another person's body as though I've done this loads of times before.

I quickly discipline my critical mind to switch off. We place more of this blue healing liquid in and around her ovaries for they feel angry, irritated and fatigued. The blue liquid dissolves the lumps around the ovaries and soothes the whole area. I hear the word "diaphragm" and then see a large rectangular black shape behind the ovaries, lower pelvis radiating all the way up to the bottom of her lower ribs, it has taken up a large part of her lower body.

I initially see what I think is light being applied to the outer line of this black shadow. As our eyes follow the outer circumference of this dark shape, I realise we are using fire. The black shadow/mass is being removed by some sort of laser burning away the outside to detach it from the body. I can't see a device, but as our eyes are following the outside of the dark mass the burning continues.

It is a very delicate procedure as we are both fixated and concentrating deeply on what we are doing. As soon as we finish, it's like we can breathe again before the black mass detaches and is sucked away into a funnel of swirling air and disappears.

No time to relax, straight back into the lady's lower pelvis and abdominal area to administer, protecting the area first with a mixture of a blue liquid substance to calm down the area. We then use our hands to push gold healing light into the area, lots of gold light.

We go back to her heart putting in more and more gold light. My guide touches her back, I touch her back and then ten, possibly twenty, loads of pairs of spiritual hands as though there is a huge team of healers working with us. I'm thinking I really hope this lady cries for she needs to release all these hidden emotions.

The beat of the drumming changes telling us we need to journey back! I'm back in the room thinking, what the hell has just happened and also knowing that what I have just done with my healing guide wasn't part of the course. As a group, we take turns to discuss what we discovered.

Oh, no! Everyone seems to have done exactly what they were told and I've gone and done something bloody different. It's my turn to share, the recipient identifies the areas we have worked on which will not be discussed and begins to cry. I feel her relief as she cries. I don't understand what has happened and nor will I pretend I do. I do know this beautiful lady has a chance of moving forwards in her life and finally will begin to heal. I truly feel content, happy, honoured and fulfilled to play a small part in helping and doing something kind for another. (I sound like I'm turning into a saint, my mum will be pleased!)

One of the course members says, "That sounds like psychic surgery you have just done." The teacher confirms not now but in the future. I knew that was what I was doing, but I wasn't going to admit to it. I have gone full circle in my life.

Eighteen years ago, I dabbled with healing, but instead of just being a channel it didn't matter how hard I tried to apply the rules, I would find myself looking inside people's bodies and would be told all their stories of emotions and hurt.

The last healing I did was on a friend who served in the military in a war zone. As I gave him healing, I saw what he had witnessed, it consisted of seeing two elderly people the soldiers had befriended laying on the floor dead covered in blood. I was upset, horrified but knew I had to continue the healing process professionally until the end.

At the end of the session, I confronted my friend who said, "That's very strange. I was just thinking about them, they were really kind people." What amused me more was that he didn't show any emotion and considered it normal.

I wish I had the knowledge of the shaman techniques as now I know I could actually do something to help him heal. Traumas in this world create ill-health within our bodies. I never really bought into this before but to have the honour to work healing for someone and then being able to physically see the shadows in front of your eyes, it is very real.

So many people have unexplained and undiagnosed illnesses, but those people know they speak the truth. I'm becoming convinced there is some truth in all of this.

FACT OR FICTION?

Throughout the course you are asked to practice your healing and gain as much experience as possible on people you think would benefit or be open to receiving healing. This results in initially asking friends and family as most people will be open to perhaps a Reiki session, but more sceptical of a shamanic healing session especially if they research it.

I believe in honesty so I try to explain that I will be assisted by the spiritual world throughout which to my surprise doesn't seem to faze anyone. I approach the most sceptical and non-believing friend I can think of as I know this person will not admit to any positive effects unless something spectacular happens. So, I arrange a date and time for this person to receive distance healing.

What do I mean by distance healing? Basically, you are not in the same room and could be miles away or even in a different country. All the person has to do is lie down and relax. The person doesn't even have to do this, but it's important they are not driving or operating heavy machinery just as a precaution.

The healing session begins and what I find fascinating is you have absolutely no idea or expectations on what is going to occur, you must remove all thoughts and allow exactly the right healing to naturally occur.

I immediately connect to my healing partner which is reassuring and comforting and dispels instantly any feelings of self-doubt. I can also see another healer observing closely.

The presence of this healer I know instantly would bring comfort to the person. I hear the word, "Discipline!" quite clearly and firmly. I automatically go back into a light trance state where you remove all thoughts, for those who are reading this that are mediums it's the same state when you are connecting with spirit but you are not working or seeking to get evidence, you are doing exactly as you are told.

As I look at the person we are healing, I discover a huge mass of darkness so large it has encased the person almost in an enormous black cloak which looks like a large shadow of stagnant slowly swirling air/cloud. My guide steps in closer and blends with my body as I'm shown images and flashbacks of this person's traumatic childhood which almost resembles clips in an old-fashioned movie.

The film is moving so quickly, but you can feel the emotions of fear, guilt, inadequacies and so many responsibilities and self-doubt for such a young child. The emotions are overwhelming which I know my guide wants me to experience and I can also sense he knows I have witnessed enough.

My guide takes over the procedure as the black shadow

of stagnant energy is vacuumed and shrunk into the palm of our hand and then removed through a funnel of swirling air into another dimension. My eyes are instantly drawn to the person's lungs where it looks inflamed and angry.

The in-depth detail inside the human body is fascinating as we are becoming submerged into the person's body. A blue swirling substance which resembles some sort of liquid form is placed into the lungs to calm down the area.

As the substance is administered, you can see the inflammation begin to settle. My eyes are drawn next to the back of the person's head. I can see a thick cord attached to the lower part of the skull and I know it has been created by past events due to extreme fear and control.

I am instructed to gently remove the cord by very gently using a twist and precise pull method and as it is removed into our hand it is sucked away into another dimension. We return to the area where we have removed the cord and insert the blue substance to calm down the site before sealing the area with a grey clay substance and then finally pushing in a healing gold light.

Every action is completed with precision checking every aspect of the work has been double checked. The intensity of the healing is serious, disciplined and professional almost as though we can't fully relax until everything has been meticulously checked.

I've worked with other healing methods which are rather pleasant and relaxing, but this method is so much more serious and precise (Just my experience!).

Finally, we check the whole body and begin increasing all the energy in each individual chakra as they have become sluggish and not allowing the full potential or the opportunity for the body to have the ability to heal itself.

We check to ensure the person is fully grounded to prevent the person from feeling woozy or just not quite balanced.

I'm starting to come out of the meditative state so I decide to go over making sure the person has been fully cleansed, grounded and protected.

I already know this has occurred, but I just feel the need for myself to ensure the person has had the full treatment (Peace of mind for me!). I'm also told quite matter of fact this person will feel better within the next few days.

Crikey! How do I explain all of that to a sceptic? I decide to tell the truth, but in perhaps a gentler approach.

The person sits there and takes it all in. The person refrains from talking about their childhood, but agrees and confirms they have led their whole life in a state of fear, guilt and an awful feeling they have never been quite good enough.

Strangely, I now feel more understanding and sympathetic why this person thinks and behaves in a certain way.

Out of all the healing that took place, the most humbling experience was to have the honour to remove that almost suffocating black cloak that this person had carried since childhood.

The emotions that we experience throughout this lifetime or perhaps in previous lifetimes really do affect our physical and mental well-being.

Not in my wildest dreams could I have imagined seeing dark shadows, cords and attachments that in my world are very real.

I actually don't know how I feel with this new insight, but I will definitely process it and then continue helping others, those that are open to it. I also decide I will not force this information on others and know in the future those that need this type of healing will be led to me.

I appreciate this world is complicated enough and think to myself would I have wanted to know all this five years ago and the answer is, certainly not, for it would have probably freaked me out!

From past experiences, I have also witnessed those that need help will find you, as whether one chooses to believe it, it's all engineered from a higher divine energy.

So, what happened to this person's health? They reluctantly mentioned they felt a little better which was a massive result, but I also had an inside source who said they had definitely been more chirpier as though a weight had been lifted from their shoulders.

I know what happened that day and I feel happy that I was able to play a small part in it. Hopefully, this person can enjoy living the rest of their life feeling happier, more content and freer without that huge burden.

Shortly after that healing session, I hear a close friend is beside herself with worry as her pet dog Albert has hurt his back. The dog has been to the vets and been given medication which he has been taking for a couple of weeks but there has been little improvement and the poor fellow is becoming lower and lower in mood.

This isn't any old dog, Albert has literally brought so much love, laughter and enjoyment back into his owner's life it really has been transformational. I can't bear to hear my friend is so upset and also the fact Albert is in a lot of pain and so miserable.

I ask my friend if she would like some healing for Albert, but explain there is no scientific proof any of this will work but I'll give it a go. "Jane, that would be wonderful, I would really appreciate it as he is so pitiful!" she said. I reiterate there is no evidence in all of this and if you don't see any improvement he has to go back to the vet, I said. Now I'm questioning myself why I have just volunteered to heal an animal! The funny thing is I already know there is no difference in sending healing to a person or an animal other than I would imagine an animal is probably less complicated emotionally and hopefully will carry less baggage.

Healing is healing and if sent with love and the right intention, surely it can help every situation if the person is receptive to it?

So, the most important thing I need to do first is ask Albert if I have permission to send him healing. I appreciate this sounds pretty mental but animal or human it is a code of conduct to seek permission.

I have never been refused permission to this day and only receive information they want discussed or need to talk about as part of their healing process.

Fascinating, how and why does this all work, the truth I don't fully understand and have got to the stage in my life where it's important to just get on with it rather than over analysing.

I have permission to proceed, put out my intention and within seconds in my healing space with my healing guide which is immediately comforting. I also notice another healer present and an advanced futuristic spiralling blue energy that looks like a mixture of air and water.

The substance is encased in a human form. I'm here to work, I'll analyse it later and then I'm straight back into my meditative, trance state. As I look at Albert, I'm drawn to his lower back. The whole of his back is swaying from side to side as though it is not connected fully to his body.

The three spiritual healers are blending so closely with me it feels as if they are literally within my body. The Indian healer is calmly leading the way bringing reassurance all of this is perfectly normal.

Two small metal bars are placed on either side of Albert's spine preventing the spine from swaying out of control.

The bars remain in position as we calm the area down once again with this blue water/air substance and you can physically see the spine settle and become strong. As soon as this is finished, I'm shown Albert's heart area where there is a congenital weakness.

We place gold energy into the area freeing up a tiny valve within the heart and I'm shown pictures and images of what I need to relay to the owner to ensure Albert has a long, healthy life. I'm then shown a dark mass of energy like a shadow.

This is nothing of concern as it has been created by

Albert and I'm shown him being bullied by another dog when he was a puppy. Yes, the other puppy was overpowering but Albert from that experience has fed the fear and anxiety by himself creating and feeding the dark shadow.

Albert has created so much fear it's like he is scared of his own shadow! I hear the word "Enough." It's time to check over Albert's body, cleanse, ground and protect. Blimey, I wasn't expecting that, gosh, it just shows I was wrong, animals carry sometimes as many hidden issues as us humans.

I told my friend what happened throughout the session reassuring her that his heart hereditary condition is not of concern, but he is to receive only one small treat a day. If she was strict with his diet he would live a long healthy life.

My friend laughed as she had just discussed with her family that they needed to reduce his treat intake. My friend listened with great intent of what had occurred and looked fascinated, but a little sceptical as any one of sound mind would.

I decided to mention the black shadow Albert had created and remarked he is literally scared of his own shadow and that I had no idea how anxious he was.

My friend burst out laughing and said, "Those words you have used to describe Albert are spot on. Jane, he really is such a woose and frightened of everything including his own shadow!"

I asked her to keep me updated on Albert's progress and then said quite matter of factly that he would feel better within a few days and be a calmer, happier and content dog. As I said those words, I felt shocked and amused as I'm not usually so direct. Where had the words come from, it was as though for a split second I was channelling my Indian guide.

I had been away for a couple of weeks on holiday and on my return my friend had contacted me to say Albert's back had improved and was so much happier and calmer.

She remarked he seemed less anxious although he still didn't like to go out in the rain. I mentioned that it wasn't any form of anxiety but intelligence.

My friend then mentioned he had been chasing a ball which he hadn't done in years. She then went quiet and thoughtful before commenting that perhaps Albert's health and behaviour might have had something to do with the healing, but sounded still unconvinced but nevertheless thanked me.

Well, I knew exactly what had happened and it didn't matter that there was no scientific explanation as Albert was back to his old self and now no longer scared of his own shadow. Many will think this is all a coincidence.

There is no such thing as a coincidence but for some this

brings comfort rather than questioning the unknown and let's face it, it makes things unexplainable easy to rationalise. What does your gut instinct tell you?

One positive thing I wanted to share was whilst healing others, I've started to notice my sensitivity to light and sound has started to improve. I sleep better and more content. It's as though I'm finally doing what I'm supposed to be doing. The fight within myself, strange choice of words has been removed.

Each time I do a healing session, I'm energised and feel strong. Gosh, I hope this continues!

DON'T CROSS THE LINE

I was asked to do a healing on a very special person who I knew needed healing, but I also knew it was or could become too personal. What do I mean by too personal? Someone that you care for so deeply you want to desperately help them and take away all their suffering.

To remain a good and physically healthy healer, you must submerge yourself in the process and detach from the person mentally to allow the natural, beautiful, healing to flow. The same as in mediumship, you are a channel for a higher source and should not allow your feelings or ego to enter.

This is hard as true mediums and healers instinctively want to heal the hurt, they can feel so intensely in others' energies. I hesitate to get involved with the healing process of this person, but also I desperately want to and how can I not help such a special person in such need?

I decide to ask my guides if I have permission and I'm immediately told I must. We arrange a date and time and I decide to put out a crystal grid to enhance the process.

What's a crystal grid? In simple terms, it's a drawn grid of lots of different lines and patterns. You choose a crystal that you are drawn to that resembles the person and place it in the middle of the grid.

As you connect with the person you intuitively pick different crystals to surround the one crystal which represents the person in the middle.

The intention of this is to think, connect and place healing crystal energy around the person.

After you have finished the healing, you can leave the grid out for the person and if you fill it is necessary place more healing energy into the grid for the person.

I can feel all the shocked crystal healers out there as I haven't done justice explaining the process. There is a lot more in-depth detail to using a crystal grid but I'm sure the majority of you don't want a full lesson on crystal grids (Apologies to anyone if offended, but I also know a lot of you wouldn't want me to retell the whole process as it's better left in the true healer's hands!).

Anyway, I don't always feel I need to use a crystal grid as it all depends on what I'm drawn to. Every person is different and unique and requires a different approach. One thing I have learnt is once you are connected to your healing partners, they know exactly what that person requires and take you straight to the right areas.

To begin with, I tried following the set and taught healing methods, but as I've said before, we are not all designed to heal in the same often mechanical procedures and nor should we. The truth is there is a higher divine pure source that needs us to channel the healing who trust me, are the true healers.

I've studied many healing methods and it all comes back to the same thing. The intention you put out has to be loving, pure and one of healing. The connection to your healers and knowing what and who you are working with I believe is vital.

The time, dedication and commitment will only strengthen your already given gifts and finally, the ability at the end to disconnect, cleanse and ground yourself.

This is where the shaman techniques are superior to any other healing method I have studied (Just my opinion!). Shamans do not mess around with working with different energies without fully protecting themselves.

The knowledge you receive at times can be brutal, but it's honest, harsh and it's the truth. I am a person who sees the good in every situation and desperately wants to believe in love, kindness and the beauty of all. The reality is unfortunately, there is good as well as evil in this world and other dimensions.

I was taught by exceptionally gifted mediums everything is about intention and nothing can harm you if you have the right loving intention. I've always inwardly known this can't be true for you can't have light without dark, yin and yang etc.

The point of this is, I have witnessed so many talented, gifted healers, mediums and lightworkers become riddled with ill health. So, the jury is out. I don't sit on the fence on this one. I now take what I do very seriously and can't afford to get it wrong.

To be able to help others you must be protected, safe and know what you are doing. I am eternally grateful for the knowledge I have been given by a talented, selfless and a real shaman healer.

What is it they say? "The right teacher will appear when the student is ready to learn." I really can't believe how ignorant I had been working at times in such extreme energy with such little knowledge on protecting myself. I feel concerned for other over excited up and coming mediums/healers who are not taught Just how important it is to protect their own energy.

I also know, whoops, I shouldn't say this, a lot of organised spiritual groups are still using old methods of protection and as my shaman teacher highlighted the vibration and the energy of this world is changing all the time and we have to change and move with it or get potentially ill and left behind. Brutal! Yes, but completely true!

I digress so I've put out my intention to connect with my healing partners to send healing to my friend.

Literally, within seconds I'm connected and bathing in a beautiful, radiant warmth of safety and bliss.

I've noticed I'm now surrounded by more healers, but

greeted by the main healer putting me at immediate ease.

The intensity is overwhelming, but reassuring and feels almost angelic, strange choice of words, but you get the picture.

My friend is in a lot of pain and asks me to have a look at specific areas of her body. The interesting thing is as I'm in the energy I'm taken to different areas of her body which looked inflamed, sore and angry which she hasn't mentioned.

I remain in the energy as my guides lead the process. We administer a blue substance best described as a mixture of water, air/wind which if the body needs changes into a sticky blue cooling gel material which I'm not sure has even been discovered yet.

What do I mean by this? I'm struggling to articulate without sounding like a fruit loop but I know it is, wait for it, futuristic! (Advanced technology! Gosh, I hope nobody ever gets to see who has written this book!) The blue substance heals the area, calms it down with some sort of cooling effect and eliminates the inflammation completely from the area.

Sparks of gold light are then placed with precision into the area which I presume for further and continual healing. As we scan the body, we repeat the process, but each area of the body is treated differently.

To an area of the body that is weak or unstable, a grey clay substance is applied with exact precision. Whilst working the atmosphere feels intense as though we are in theatre performing an almost surgical procedure that must be perfect.

There is no acceptance or time for incompetence or error. The guides I'm working with have done this thousands of times and literally just need me to channel their work. Whilst working, they are allowing me to witness everything, why? It will become apparent in the future I have absolutely no doubt.

The whole process is fascinating as I have learnt and studied the human body in my past career which enables me to know and identify the different parts of the body. Who would have known all that previous studying would have come back in use? No such thing as a coincidence!

We continue to scan the body adding and increasing the energy. I've noticed with a lot of people that for whatever reason, their energy can become stagnant. Energy within the body needs to move freely to enable the body the optimal chance of healing itself. Again, my guides show me a technique to get the energy to move properly without restriction.

The energy needs not only to move at the right frequency/speed, but also each chakra needs to synchronise with the rest of the body at the right speed for the individual person. I'm honoured and relieved that they are allowing me the insight, but also I'm not deluded that they are the ones with the expertise and running the show (Thank goodness, that's a bloody relief!).

As we continue, I suddenly desperately feel I need to help this person and can feel my energy depleting. I'm so eager to help this person, I'm giving all I have. The connection stops, nothing! Black, I can no longer see inside the body! I have lost all connection with my healers.

I stood there thinking first of all what to do and secondly trying to regain the connection. I'm connected back to my guides and firmly told, "Jane, you are part of this, you are not running this. Step back and allow us to use the energy. Do you understand?"

My main guide spoke with such authority and firmness there was no way I could misunderstand what I was being told. I quickly learnt from that experience I was forbidden to give my energy away and needed to detach emotionally from the healing. I was a channel and part of a team, nothing more, nothing less.

If I didn't listen, they had the power to pull the plug and would. I felt not only protected but also really emotional that I had such a caring team who would not allow me to become ill. Knowing that healing others would not affect my health was a huge relief because it had secretly been one of my concerns and worries.

The penny had finally dropped! I needed to stop questioning the process and just get on with it! Literally, as soon as I thought these words the connection of healing with my team was switched back on and I was back looking inside the human body.

I removed all feelings and emotions and suddenly became this professional medical healer who had a serious job to do.

I accepted the importance of my role within the team and I had no right to hinder their job by bringing in human vulnerabilities.

I potentially could have been the weak link in the process, but fortunately my guides would under no circumstances allow this to happen and if necessary cut off our connection.

Although the lesson was harsh, I was thankful this had happened for I knew in the future I was protected, safe and they would not allow me to become ill. If a healer gives away all their energy to help another, inevitably, they will become depleted.

Once the healing session was completed, I followed through with strict shaman protection, cleansing and grounding rituals on the person and then myself.

As a medium in the past, it could take hours for the

symptoms of the person being channelled through to leave your body.

For example, if somebody had had a stroke before passing over, you would be walking around with a numbness on the left side of your face which was pretty awful, especially the first few times before you were aware of where it was coming from.

In my early days, I would ask more experienced mediums for advice on how to remove these sensations and they would simply reply I just needed to be more disciplined and not allow this to happen.

 What the hell does that mean? So, I would shut up, stop moaning and just walk around with other people's ailments attached to me which often took hours to leave my body (Not nice!).

I would use all different techniques, but none that actually worked. In the end, you became less bothered with the strange physical symptoms of deceased others as you knew it would pass. Different spiritual techniques need to be explored and shared to protect everyone who is called to do spiritual work to help others. I've just had a little laugh as I know of many spiritual organisations who wouldn't be keen on welcoming shaman practises and I also know Shamans that wouldn't want to work in what they consider the middle world, lower energy.

So funny! Then you have what people consider normal,

the more traditional religions. The so-called normal religions would shudder at any other religion other than their own. I believe there is a higher, beautiful and divine energy that we can all access if we choose.

The kindest and most selfless people I have come across often believe in nothing and whether they want to believe it or not, are the most connected to the divine source for they are living loving and kind lives.

I also have a feeling that divine energy doesn't care what we choose to believe or follow and has no intention of us abiding by often man-made rules, but just wants us to be loving, kind and caring to one another.

Us humans are often so judgmental and have an unwilling ability to accept all. I have this positive hope for the future that the younger generation will start to work things out for themselves and become more accepting of all.

I digressed, back to the original healing session. Once I have completed the healing, I then ring up the person who has had healing and we discuss what I found or felt.

These words are chosen very carefully and explained differently for each person. The whole idea is to heal the person, not scare the hell out of them. Anyway, the person I have just sent healing to is fascinated and open-minded so I can speak more freely.

The person confirms the areas we have been working on have been causing her great discomfort, but not as severe as her main injuries. This is where I completely trust in my healing partners that they know exactly what is right for the person. We then had a serious chat about a cord I removed which was attached to a past situation which had affected her whole life on how she perceived every new and challenging event.

What detrimental things we hear repeatedly as children develop our thinking. The conversation went from being intrigued to sadness, tears and finally acceptance and healing. The power of sharing and a safe environment to finally talk openly and allow past events to be processed and acknowledged could finally be laid to rest.

Those cords had been detached but needed to almost be validated so not only the physical but the mental could heal. It blows my mind the intelligence of the spiritual world. They make no mistakes, they are highly emotionally, spiritually and far more intelligent than us mere humans.

At the end of the conversation, I truly felt humbled, honoured and knew whatever the outcome of my friend's healing journey, she no longer carried the weight of her childhood beliefs upon her shoulders. I learnt another valuable lesson.

Sometimes in life, you must cross uncomfortable lines

to help others, but never at the expense of your health!

THE COURSE RANKS UP A GEAR

The course continues to feed my thirst for knowledge and at the same time blows the logical side of my brain to smithereens. What we experience and witness on the course has no scientific proof, but somehow works and is incredibly powerful.

Initially, after each teaching session, I would spend long periods quietly going over what I had just seen, sensed and felt. Everything felt so natural, normal and gave me a sense of comfort and belonging. How could this be? I had never used any of these methods or been taught them before, but before the teacher had finished speaking the words, I already knew the outcome and exactly what to do.

My mind felt uneasy, a little fragile if I am going to be completely honest and I started behaving over analytical with repetitive thoughts on why and how all of these shaman techniques could work. I inwardly knew the answer to all my questions, but my logic kept fighting the reality of this world.

Another telling off was overdue by my spiritual team. I had a decision to make. Option one, lose the plot trying to unravel and understand why I was able to do things that I hadn't even got the imagination to do or pick option two.

Option two pull myself together, get on with the new

techniques, and accept I didn't need to understand everything. The ultimate goal was to help people heal and I was no good to anyone if I couldn't mentally hold it together.

The words the spirit world used for my reality check were firm, harsh and authoritative which was exactly what I needed to hear. The choice of words used gave me clarity, strength and an immediate understanding and comfort on moving forwards.

All fear and apprehension on delving deeper into the shamanic world disappeared; it was literally a light bulb moment.

It was a good job as the course became more extreme as we ventured into deeper realms to retrieve information to help heal people, but were also taught procedures to protect ourselves.

What people don't realise is a true shaman goes to spiritual environments that most people wouldn't even entertain to help perhaps retrieve a soul part lost from a past life or this life. Why? I hear you think.

So that the person who they are healing can become complete, whole, enabling them to have a more fulfilling and happier journey on earth. Wacky, right? Yes, but true. Completely selfless and ballsy if you ask me!

SOUL RETRIEVAL – FACT OR FICTION?

I would never discuss the procedures of performing a soul retrieval as this I personally believe needs to be taught by an experienced shaman. A true honourable shaman would not teach this to a person who wasn't ready for the procedure and to be honest I would not recommend it to anyone unless it was their calling.

I would also question why a person would need to do this unless it was to help another. I laugh as I say this as before this course, I would have run a mile from anything to do with shamanism.

I've had lots of spiritual adventures and surprises, but I really never thought in my wildest dreams I would even contemplate doing this. As I have said before, if the spirit world has chosen you to work in a specific way, it will happen. I have complicated my journey by refusing to listen.

I have gone off several times exploring what I think to be more exciting and fulfilling, but I'm always brought back to exactly where I should be. It genuinely puzzles me still to this day why they didn't pick someone more compliant.

My journey could have run so much smoother if I had listened to my guides who have told me numerous times my story has already been written. Trust, patience and of course love, are the key to harmony and happiness.

That annoying word patience! I have proven the spirit world to be right so many times with my desire to push through this life a hundred miles an hour. Well, I got there in the end, although I'm not deluded, I'm sure I will still make more mistakes.

Making mistakes isn't a bad thing, a bit exhausting and in my case a bit repetitive, but eventually when the time is right, you'll learn. On a positive note, if I hadn't made so many mistakes what would I have been able to write about? Nothing worse than hearing bullshit about how perfect a person's life is (Just my unspiritual opinion!).

As a channel writer, I'm often told certain situations in the future are going to change. For example, a change of job or moving home. What fascinates me is how these things are engineered to perfection by a more intelligent source. I look back on my life and know I haven't fallen into situations, met the right people at the right time. I would be very closed minded to presume all of this was a coincidence.

As I have said, I will not reveal the shaman retrieval techniques, but I will share my experience with you. This is just my experience but if you haven't already come up with the conclusion, in society I would be considered a little unconventional and to most unacceptable, I have a strong feeling after reading the next paragraph, you might be about to change your mind.

Here goes, sorry, mum!

What do I mean by soul retrieval? Basically, a part of the person you are treating has lost a part of their soul perhaps due to trauma or from what I have experienced so far tends to be from a childhood memory that the child can't cope with, perhaps a messy divorce, moving home, sexual abuse, the list goes on.

The shaman teacher used a better example which is, sometimes, if a person has been in a car accident due to pain and shock, the person literally can't remember or detaches from the situation. This can sometimes result in a part of the soul being detached which would make sense if any of this does as the body would immediately go into protecting the body.

The technique is only used if you are guided to by your spiritual team. The whole point of this, I hear your thoughts. My interpretation is that if the person is whole, this journey will be a more positive experience and enable the person to heal whether it be physical, mental, or spiritual. If a person has lost a part of their soul which can also be from previous lives, this journey could feel more difficult and not as fulfilling. People who have had soul retrievals done on them can't usually explain why, but they feel more content, happier and accepting of themselves in the here and now. A positive reaction but once again I am aware there is no scientific evidence or proof.

Yes, I will admit I questioned this at first as there is no logical proof to any of this and secondly at the time I wasn't overly excited about journeying to the lower world to retrieve parts of people's souls. When I first heard we were going to do this, not only did I think this was extreme and surely if the person hadn't missed that part of their soul then we should perhaps just leave everything be and not mess around with the unknown.

The more I learnt about the procedure, I came to realise that a lot of people are unable to get better due to not being fully connected to themselves. I have this inner overwhelming desire to heal the whole person. What is the point in healing if you only do the nice and easy bits? If healing methods are going to be effective, you have to treat the whole person and that means delving deeper.

At this point, the whole shaman healing approach changed rapidly.

Journeying to the lower world was initially blissful, but now if I'm being truthful, I could see possibly a more extreme and powerful side to it.

There was so much more to the lower world. A fascinating world where there are no limitations including retrieving lost soul parts of others. From the beginning of the course I hadn't bought into the fluffy side of the lower world and knew we would only be given access to shaman techniques if our teacher believed first of all we had the ability to help others and secondly we could cope with it.

I did question my own abilities and felt a little fearful, but was told firmly by my spiritual team this was part of my journey and I was a hundred percent protected. There are set procedures and techniques you are taught which need to be strictly adhered to. Trust me, once you hear what you are doing and how you need to retrieve a soul part, you hang onto every word. We are no longer playing, we are travelling to other realms and there is no guarantee what we will see, feel, sense and have to deal with.

We were also warned that we might come across a soul thief and have to persuade them to return the soul part back to us. What is a soul thief? Good question. In my words, an energy, entity or thing that I genuinely don't know what it will look like until I come across it. If this was to happen you have to negotiate by offering gifts from your healing and retrieval toolkit.

Some shamans will go straight in and if necessary steal back the soul part. We were taught this is not the best method as the soul thief will simply come back and steal the soul part again. Crikey! Too much to process!

At this point, I had a little nervous giggle as I thought I

was on the wrong course and part of Hogwarts! Why would you do this? It sounds not only dangerous, but stupid to risk your safety for another person who would have no appreciation of what you were doing for them.

That's exactly what I thought. So, why? A deeper passion and fire lit within to heal, that's basically it! The funny thing is, we were taught what we could come across, nothing was flowered up and it was all brutally honest but somewhere along the way I had lost all fear. I identified this as strange and a little amusing, but almost felt like some sort of empowered warrior who feared nothing. I had a deep knowing I had once again done all of this before.

Each time I connected with my spiritual team, I became rapidly more confident and accepting. As I have said, I will not discuss the teaching techniques but I will tell you before we went journeying we were taken to different realms to connect to our soul retrieval power animal's including power and protection.

We were also taught different scenarios so hopefully not to feel shocked by anything, but there was no guarantee. When I first heard this, as usual, I was sceptical but I had full knowledge and trusted our teacher. I disciplined my mind and committed fully to the journey.

The first thing was to connect to our soul retrieval power animal. I noticed on this journey we travelled deeper and deeper down dark tunnels to what felt like nearer the centre of earth. I know this sounds ridiculous but this was my experience!

Finally, the journey stopped and I stood barefooted having a look around. The first thing I see is a large male tiger close by my side. I've never seen a tiger other than in books and find myself mesmerised by how large it is and how powerful, lean and muscular its body looks.

It's so beautiful, striking, graceful, yet I respect it is also unpredictable and if he should choose, savage and deadly. I have no fear for I know we work as one and the tiger has accepted me as one of his own.

Our eyes are locked staring deep into one another's dark pupils again exploring the true depths of one another's souls. The intensity of our gaze is so powerful, strong, familiar and yet comforting. I feel totally at ease and safe.

As I stroke the tiger, I can feel the smooth, glossy fur within my fingers and the warmth of the animal. I notice and can feel the gentle movement of the tiger's lungs inhaling and exhaling calmly against my hand. As we become closer, our bodies start to merge into one. I suddenly feel a heightened sensation of power, control, strength and almighty.

I am courageous and all harm is immediately eradicated. I can't be harmed for I have become protection and power itself. The intensity is making me feel lightheaded and woozy so I decide to withdraw out of the tiger's body, returning back to standing by the side of the tiger gently stroking and gazing into this beautiful, powerful, animal's eyes.

I hear the beat of the drum changing, this signals it's time to journey back. I say my goodbyes, feeling a little sad to be leaving, but I know I will be working alongside this beautiful, powerful and almost mystical creature very soon. Once back into the material world, I feel emotionally overwhelmed.

My logical mind starts overworking trying to work out how I could have felt such real intensity. The ability to touch, feel and sense what felt truly physical and as though in the material world. I felt the tiger's fur, the warmth of its body and witnessed the sensation of the lungs actually moving. Not only that, we allowed one another access completely into each other's souls.

No hidden agenda, all aspects, truth and honesty including my inner darker fears lay bare for this creature to fully understand me and what he would be working with. We share our experiences among the group and I openly admit I need time to process the intensity of all of this. I'm very good at compartmentalising things, but I also appreciate that I need time to process and not rush through this one.

The following week, we are given tasks to do daily to

explore the soul retrieval method and must learn and make sure we are not only confident, but comfortable to work on another person. My logical brain says the course has been an eye-opener, but really this is too far and possibly dangerous if not administered properly so, no thanks.

Why would you do this? The answer keeps coming back to helping others. I'm certainly not a holy saint-like person and the day if ever I should become all angelic and no longer relatable then, please will someone out there have a firm word with me!

I decide I not only want to do it, but have this inner hunger and desire, when needed to retrieve a lost part of a person's soul to make them complete. Yikes!

The next few days I study meticulously exactly the procedure I must adhere to. I spend time journeying mostly to the upper world connecting with my healing team to be shown and given protection methods and devices. I personally find (This is different for everyone) journeying to the upper world is straight to the point, no nonsense or symbolic symbols to work out, just straight talking and honesty.

Don't get me wrong, you don't always get what you want to hear and it's certainly not flowered up, or fluffy but for me, I like simplicity and straight talking. The spirit world knows how we work best and I believe we work to our strengths. We are given nothing in this life we can't handle however challenging our journeys can seem at times. I'll admit at times I can be a bit of a control freak and if I'm going to do soul retrieval then I need to be prepared as best I can.

I know I can't be fully prepared for you will not know what you are going to find until you journey into other realms, but it makes me feel like I have some form of control which for me helps. It also helps that my spirit team has never in my entire life let me down.

I have messed up as you know several times, but my guides have always protected and kept me safe.

I made the decision that before I do a soul retrieval on another person, I need to do a soul retrieval on myself. I don't know whether you even can, but I'm going to explore it as I need to know if it is safe to use on others.

I'm not keen on revealing this experience, but have been told by my spirit team I have to, so here goes. I send out my intention that I will journey to the lower world to connect to my retrieval power animal to see if there is a soul part that is willing to return to me at this time. I put myself into a trance state and follow the set procedures we have been taught.

Within seconds, I am flying down dark tunnels going deeper and deeper into the lower world. I'm surprised at how quickly I have arrived into the lower world and immediately first feel the presence of tiger and then see him quite clearly. I feel relieved and immediately empowered and protected.

We travel further deeper into the lower world in search of any missing soul parts. Within seconds we stop, we have arrived at the right location.

I notice the tiger is standing a little further away as though observing rather than protecting me. I look around and see a little girl, she is about nine or ten years old, pretty, mousy brown hair and freckles. It's me! I'm staring at myself as a child. I'm startled and then discipline myself and remember why I am here.

As I look at myself as a child, I find myself being nurturing, loving and kind. I feel overwhelmed with the feeling I want to protect her and make her feel safe. I couch down and ask her why she is here. She replies, "I'm so scared of everything and don't belong in this world."

I'm then shown a black and white film of childhood memories I had completely forgotten. I see clips of adults making her feel inadequate, school memories of heightened fear and such a deep sense of being born at the wrong time in the wrong place. A disconnection with her surroundings, not feeling loved and understood fully.

As I'm looking at this child, I explain who I am and that she is my younger self. I assure her I still at times feel a little bit wobbly, but I'm not scared of anything anymore as I've learnt to accept who I am and we can help others to feel safe too. I tell her I'm a kind, loving and gentle person and if she wishes she can come back with me. I will look after her, protect her and she will no longer feel different or unconnected as we are to be reconnected as one.

She looks at me intensely and nods her head and says, "I'm so tired of feeling scared and lonely and would like to come back with you." I follow the procedure to ensure every aspect of her soul is retrieved. I check over and over again ensuring I have done everything correctly for my mothering instincts are heightened and I will not allow this child to suffer anymore.

Her soul is within me, I journey back with the protection of the tiger until we part ways. As soon as I return back to the material world, I ensure the soul is within me safely. I check my entire body, sealing certain areas and then decide to seal everything followed by cleansing and protection.

I forgot to ask my younger self what gifts were returned to me because this procedure was about the child's needs and didn't feel right to question her about my adult needs. My guides confirmed the gifts returned were finally freedom and trust! Did that just happen?

Here goes the logical side of my brain again. It just happened! I had just had a conversation with my nine-year-old self. I felt sad for my younger self, shed quite a few tears, and then felt the luckiest woman alive, to be able to have the gift to reconnect that child back to where she belonged. I found the whole process profound. As a child, I must have become so overwhelmed by certain situations I disconnected and literally lost parts of my soul. I initially questioned the reality of this procedure, but now I couldn't for I had just witnessed this for myself.

After that soul retrieval, I experienced recurring memories of my childhood, how I felt from the child's perspective which I had previously locked away. It was like some sort of therapy where I had to revisit and acknowledge the child's feelings and why. I can't say it was a pleasant experience, but I also knew I had an obligation to myself as a child.

I can honestly say after a week or so I genuinely felt much happier, content, calmer and more okay as a person! I'm not usually into this type of gentle, fluffy approach, especially being ex-military but I'm not ignorant enough to turn my back on the opportunity to heal. Some things in life can't yet be explained, but that doesn't mean it isn't real.

THE DAY HAS ARRIVED

The day has arrived where we will be putting all our knowledge and healing skills to the test whilst being closely monitored by our shaman teacher. I have so much respect for our teacher as her values and morals are incredibly high and she has such a desire to share all her gifts selflessly to the best of her ability.

Other healing methods I have studied tend to be taught in a one-size-fits-all, but with the shaman method the healer is identified as an individual and is given the freedom and encouraged to work with their true gifts. I believe strongly that if you are a true healer, in time and with experience, you will find your own technique and if working as a direct channel you have to trust and basically become submerged in the process.

The spirit world, a higher divine energy, whatever you feel comfortable calling it, is ultimately in control. Some will disagree with this opinion, but from a life of working with a higher divine energy the best healing results for the patient come from surrendering your ego and yourself to the process. It takes a lot of discipline and courage, but that's when the healing is at its strongest.

I'm feeling a little apprehensive going into the unknown, but also have this overwhelming feeling of confidence, courage and strength. I again don't know where or when I have gained this but it's empowering and I decide I'm going to embrace and enjoy every second of it for I'm not sure how long it will last.

We are allocated a person each and our shaman teacher watches over our every move to ensure we follow the set procedure correctly. Once we are comfortable with the set procedures, she knows each and every one of us will be guided slightly differently with different approaches and techniques.

The healers sit in the silence before beginning the journey to the lower world. I'm journeying fast deeper into the lower world where I'm immediately met by my soul retrieval animal, Tiger. The strength and power of this beautiful, mystical creature, blends within me as I instantaneously become fearless. I feel courageous, powerful and have an animalistic hunger to go in search of any soul parts that are happy to be retrieved for my client.

As one, we travel deeper until we come to an abrupt stop. Tiger withdraws further behind me allowing my tender side to step forward. I see a child who looks like the spitting image of my client and I immediately know it is her, but I also need to check. I crouch down low looking into the face of a pretty, blonde haired and blue-eyed girl who looks about five years old.

She looks amused to see me. As I look at her, attached to her left hand is a dark shadow substance in the form of a young boy. I know from experience this is a child in spirit that is no longer permitted access to the material world. I'm initially shocked as we hadn't covered this, but then I feel an overwhelming presence of my healing team stepping in as though leading the way.

I feel a calmness of love and inner peace sweep through my entire body as I proceed with the process. I ask the little girl why she is here and she explains she feels sad, not safe and frightened. The little girl explains the adults are all so sad because she overheard the adults talking about a little boy who had recently died. "They won't say who he is, but I feel their deep sadness, my tummy feels so horrible as though I want to be sick. I can't stop feeling all this scary dark sadness within me.

I can't cope with the sicky feeling and sadness in my body and around me. I want to cry, but I can't. I don't know what to do, I can't talk about it as I shouldn't have been listening," the child said. I reassure her that her feelings are okay as that is very sad. I explain who I am and that if it is okay with her we can stop all this sadness and return her to her grown up self which will make her feel safe, belonged and loved.

She asks me what the lady is like that she will be returning to. I tell her the truth. The lady is fun, kind, loving and will protect you and yes, she is very pretty just like you. The little girl seems happy to return but first I have to address the spirit child attached to her left hand.

I explain to the little girl it is time to let go of your friend for he will be happier to stay here and by detaching him he will be able to return to where he needs to be just like you. She hesitates and then looks me in the eye and says in a quiet gentle voice, "Okay."

I lean forward and place my hand on her left hand before very gently rotating the dark shadow substance in a precise, gentle, almost clicking sensation. The shadow vanishes into thin air. I double checked scanning the whole body of the little girl to make sure there is nothing else attached to her. "She is clear. Enough," I hear my healing spirit guide say. It's time to take her back to her current self. I gather up the energy of the little girl making a scooping action with my hands into a crystal that remains close to my heart. Tiger steps in closer as we all travel back towards the middle world.

We leave Tiger at a set location before travelling to the material world. I'm back in the room in a lighter trance state following all the procedures to ensure this soul is firmly and safely put back into the patient.

The soul is transferred back to the person through the crown chakra, top of the head and the heart chakra, the heart area. It's the most beautiful thing to witness as you feel, sense and see a part of the person's soul return. Sounds ridiculous but is like watching a miracle of life return.

As soon as the soul part is returned, the work continues

ensuring the energy of the patient is sealed, cleansed and finally protected. Once the procedure is complete, you can then inform the person of what happened and what gifts, talents and strengths have been returned; that's if the client is open-minded enough to receive the information.

Not every person who decides to have a shamanic healing treatment will want to know what has occurred. As the healer, you have to judge what each person can cope with. The most important thing is to heal the person, not blow their mind with the technicalities.

At the end of the soul retrieval session, the shaman is pleased with all of us, but identifies I used a slightly different technique which she hadn't seen before but was happy as she also witnessed the soul part return safely and securely into the person.

I honestly thought I had followed every procedure exactly as taught, but whilst in a light trance working with my team, I had become submerged in their approach. My shaman teacher was delighted with us all and reassured me my approach had achieved exactly the right outcome. I love the fact this specific shaman teacher is so advanced spiritually she automatically gets told by her own team what is acceptable and when to intervene.

I can honestly say that the soul retrieval experience blew my mind. Logical brain coming in asking questions, how could that have happened, but it did. I revisited that soul retrieval healing and discussed it over with another healer on the course which enabled both of us the ability to stop over analysing the shaman techniques.

We had been proven time and time again these methods enabled us to be better prepared for anything any patient could bring to us. We also knew that possibly in the future we wouldn't get those who needed a little bit of gentle healing, but needed extreme help and healing. Let's face it, if you want a little bit of gentle healing and perhaps your chakras, energy energised you probably wouldn't go in search for someone who has learnt shaman healing techniques.

I laugh at this comment as before I literally fell onto this path there is no way in the world I would have gone to a shaman due to my preconceived view of shamanism. If you research what a shaman does it can be perceived as a dark method of healing whilst working with the spirit world. I would argue this point now as a true lightworker who uses these techniques is pretty ballsy and selfless to go journeying for another human being in the hope of healing and making them whole.

There is good and bad in every discipline as we have historically found in all walks of life including established religions and professional organisations. I often find those who judge the most tend to forget and sweep under the carpet their personal associations with historical corruption in some of their chosen beliefs. Anyway, it's not for any of us to judge one another.

If we choose to judge, at least make it on facts, not fiction and simply man-made fears. I will admit I had fears of shamanism, but now I respect and keep an open mind. I have been fortunate and honoured to meet a true shaman, but I'm also not deluded that there will be good as well as bad for this tends to be a human flaw and one at present we can't seem to eradicate.

What is the saying? It only takes a few rotten apples!

SO, WHAT IS NEXT?

The six-week intensive course has finally come to an end and to be honest, I'm relieved to step away and have some time to reflect. I can honestly say I have never learnt so much in such a short period of time. I have learnt different and traditional shaman methods on how to cleanse spaces and protect myself, the patient and the surroundings.

I have journeyed to the lower world and higher world which I initially had no appreciation or understanding of and to be totally honest didn't even know existed. More importantly, this course has taught me I am stronger and braver than what I could have imagined.

Through the selfless guidance and knowledge of a true shaman, I discovered the correct realm I needed to work in with my spiritual healing team to help others. I now know how to access different realms if and when I am called upon to use them.

Shamanism is not only an incredibly powerful, healing method, but reconnects you to nature and what is really important in this life. So, what is the importance of this life? Back to basics –nature, nurture, love, healing and a desire to help one another. That's it in a nutshell.

After the course,I continued to use the shaman methods in my healing but quickly noticed I was taken to a different realm that gives me access to techniques that I know full well are not shaman techniques. The shaman course has eliminated my fear of the unknown. I have a wealth of knowledge and techniques to add to my healing tool kit.

I am eternally grateful to have met a genuine shaman who has given me access to where and how I should be working. I have gone on to do healing and have come across times, where I have been faced with having to retrieve a soul part to enable a person the ability to fully heal. Would I have been able to do this before studying shamanism?

The strange answer is yes, as I know I have done this all before in perhaps another life, but would I have been brave enough? Probably not! The shaman teacher gave me the most precious gift of all, self belief, confidence, courage and access to the protection and power of a tiger.

I feel so lucky, blessed and grateful. I will continue the healing method my spiritual team has chosen me to do, but in the future I will continue to study and practise when called upon other shaman techniques. Some healing institutes are not keen on mixing healing methods and some organisations forbid it.

This blows my mind. As a healer, the patients' needs come first and they are all different. A true healer will be guided to use whatever methods they are guided to use and should at no cost listen to controlling human ideology.

Healers simply need to trust and listen purely to the higher divine energy they have been chosen to work in. It flabbergasts me how ignorant man is when it comes to healing and helping another.

On a positive note, I feel more grounded, energised and I've also noticed after each healing session I receive healing from the spirit world when I return to be cleansed. It's as though the spirit world acknowledges every time you give your energy to help another, they repay you with their love and healing.

After each healing session I feel alive, healthy and happy but most of all honoured to be given access to work as part of an advanced healing team to help another. So, the jury is out, is what I have revealed a lot of nonsense to put it politely or is there truth in these words?

You, the reader, will have to decide for yourself. Some of you will already know the truth and be able to resonate and others perhaps a little baffled. Both are fine if nothing else. I hope I have opened your minds and given you another way of viewing this beautiful and unassuming world.

FAREWELL FOR NOW

What am I doing at present? Within days of completing the shaman course, I was contacted by a friend of a friend to help heal a person who is terminally ill and had been stripped of all hope. My friend said, "I'd been racking my brains to find a healer who doesn't heal in the normal way and then you popped into my head." I laughed as I couldn't work out whether that was supposed to be a compliment or not.

She reassured me it was a compliment as so- called normal healing wasn't going to be strong enough. I asked my guides for their blessing and was told I had to and that it had been engineered.

So, currently I'm working with my healing team using techniques again I didn't know existed, but I no longer question. I know I am part of something more powerful, loving and healing than me and just honoured if nothing else to return hope to another.

I have also been told this book has to be released as soon as possible to hit the right timelines. What does this mean, I have my suspicions as I have been given glimpses into the future, but I really don't want to know.

My health has improved and I become stronger and stronger each day, but I'm also aware I can't run before I can walk. I have been told numerous times by my spirit team that my health will make a full recovery and I have had it explained in frank, firm words that apparently, I had agreed to this journey and to write about it before I came to earth.

Surely, I wasn't that stupid! Well, it seems I must have been. I know full well that if I hadn't experienced ill health, there would be no way with my personality I would be sitting down on a computer writing a badly written book. So perhaps there might be some truth in it?

Spoiler alert! I have my suspicions there will be one more final book to the reluctant medium series. What about, I don't know yet. Secretly, I'd rather go back to channel writing but that's not how it works when you agree to work for the spirit world. I will be led to what I need to do next, but hopefully next time, I'll be able to tell you my health has made a full recovery and I'm bouncing around being a complete pain in the arse. I can't wait!

To all those people struggling whether that be physically, mentally, or spiritually, remember these words: "We are given nothing in this life we cannot deal with, nothing can stay the same forever and finally, everything every day gets better, better and better.

Printed in Great Britain
by Amazon

42868143R00195